SHAKESPEARE

JULIUS CAESAR

NOTES

COLES EDITORIAL BOARD

Publisher's Note

Otabınd (Ota-bind). This book has been bound
using the patented Otabind process. You can
open this book at any page, gently run your
finger down the spine, and the pages will lie flat.

Bound to stay open

ABOUT COLES NOTES

COLES NOTES have been an indispensible aid to students on five continents since 1948.

COLES NOTES are available for a wide range of individual literary works. Clear, concise explanations and insights are provided along with interesting interpretations and evaluations.

Proper use of COLES NOTES will allow the student to pay greater attention to lectures and spend less time taking notes. This will result in a broader understanding of the work being studied and will free the student for increased participation in discussions.

COLES NOTES are an invaluable aid for review and exam preparation as well as an invitation to explore different interpretive paths.

COLES NOTES are written by experts in their fields. It should be noted that any literary judgement expressed herein is just that – the judgement of one school of thought. Interpretations that diverge from, or totally disagree with any criticism may be equally valid.

COLES NOTES are designed to supplement the text and are not intended as a substitute for reading the text itself. Use of the NOTES will serve not only to clarify the work being studied, but should enhance the readers enjoyment of the topic.

ISBN 0-7740-3199-9

© COPYRIGHT 2006 AND PUBLISHED BY
COLES PUBLISHING COMPANY
TORONTO - CANADA
PRINTED IN CANADA

Manufactured by Webcom
Cover finish: Webcom's Exclusive **DURACOAT**

CONTENTS

Characters

Meaning

Style

WILLIAM SHAKESPEARE LIFE AND WORKS

Biographical Sketch

With the epithet "Dear Son of Memory", Milton praised Shakespeare as one constantly in our memories and brother of the Muses. Certainly no other author has held such sway over the literary world, undiminished through some three and a half centuries of shifting artistic tastes. Shakespeare's plots and his characters have continued to be a living reality for us; as his well known contemporary Ben Jonson wrote, in a familiar tribute, "Thou . . . art alive still, while thy Booke doth live,/ And we have wits to read, and praise to give."

The Early Years

Despite such acclaim and the scholarship it has spawned, our knowledge of Shakespeare's life is sketchy, filled with more questions than answers, even after we prune away the misinformation accumulated over the years. He was baptized on April 26, 1564, in Holy Trinity Church, Stratford-on-Avon. As it was customary to baptize children a few days after birth, we conjecture that he was born on April 23. The monument erected in Stratford states that he died on April 23, 1616, in his fifty-third year.

William was the third child of John Shakespeare, who came to Stratford from Snitterfield before 1532 as a "whyttawer" (tanner) and glover, and Mary Arden, daughter of a wealthy "gentleman of worship" from Wilmecote. They married around 1557. Since John Shakespeare owned one house on Greenhill Street and two on Henley Street, we cannot be certain where William was born, though the Henley Street shrine draws many tourists each year. William's two older sisters died in infancy, but three brothers and two other sisters survived at least into childhood.

Shakespeare's father was fairly well-to-do, dealing in farm products and wool, and owning considerable property in Stratford. After holding a series of minor municipal offices he was elected alderman in 1565, high bailiff (roughly similar to the mayor of today) in 1568, and chief alderman in 1571. There are no records of young Will Shakespeare's education (though there are many unfounded legends), but he undoubtedly attended the town school maintained by the burgesses, which prepared its students for the universities. Ben Jonson's line about Shakespeare's having "small *Latine*, and lesse *Greeke*" refers not to his education but to his lack of indebtedness to the classical writers and dramatists.

On November 27, 1582, a licence to marry was issued to "Willelmum Shaxpere *et* Annam Whateley *de* Temple Grafton," and on

1

the next day a marriage bond for "Willm Shagspere" and "Anne Hathwey of Stratford" was signed by Fulk Sandells and John Richardson, farmers of Stratford. This bond stated that there was no "lawful let or impediment by reason of any precontract, consanguinity, affinity, or by any other lawful means whatsoever"; thus "William and Anne (were) to be married together with once asking of the banns of matrimony." The problem of Anne Whateley has led many researchers and some detractors to argue all kinds of improbabilities, such as the existence of two different Shakespeares and the forging of documents to conceal Shakespeare's true identity. The actual explanation seems to be simple: the clerk who made the marriage licence entry apparently copied the name "Whateley" from a preceding entry, as a glance at the full sheet suggests. (Incidentally, Nicholas Rowe in his life of Shakespeare, published in 1709, well before the discovery of these marriage records, gave Anne's name as Hathaway.) The problems of marriage with Anne Hathaway — he was eighteen and she was twenty-six — and of the bond have caused similar consternation. Why did these two marry when there was such a discrepancy of age? Why only one saying of the banns (rather than the usual three)? Why the emphasis on a possible legal impediment? The answer here is not simple or definite, but the birth of a daughter Susanna, baptized at Holy Trinity on May 26, 1583, seems to explain the odd circumstances. It should be recognized, however, that an engagement to marry was considered legally binding in those days (we still have breach-of-promise suits today) and that premarital relations were not unusual or frowned upon when an engagement had taken place. The circumstances already mentioned, Shakespeare's ensuing activities, and his will bequeathing to Anne "my second best bed with the furniture" have suggested to some that their marriage was not entirely happy. Their other children, the twins Hamnet and Judith, were christened on February 2, 1585.

Theatrical Life

Shakespeare's years before and immediately after the time of his marriage are not charted, but rumor has him as an apprentice to a master butcher or as a country teacher or an actor with some provincial company. He is supposed to have run away from whatever he was doing for livelihood and to have gone to London, where he soon attached himself to some theatrical group. At this time there were only two professional houses established in the London environs, The Theatre (opened in 1576) and The Curtain (opened in 1577). His first connection with the theater was reputedly as holder of horses; that is, one of the stage crew, but a most inferior assignment. Thereafter he became an actor (perhaps at this time he met Ben Jonson), a writer, and a director. Such experience had its mark in the theatricality of his plays. We do know that he was established in London by 1592, when Robert Greene lamented in *A Groatsworth of Wit* (September, 1592) that professional actors had gained priority in the theater over university-trained writers like himself: "There is an upstart Crow, beautified with our feathers, that with his *Tygers hart wrapt in a Players hyde*, supposes he is as well able to bombast out a lanke verse as the best of you: and beeing an absolute *Iohannes fac totum* (Jack-of-all-trades), is in his owne conceit the onely Shake-scene in a countrey." An apology for Greene's ill-humored statement by Henry Chettle, the editor of the pamphlet, appeared around December 1592 in *Kind-Hart's Dream*.

Family Affairs

To return to the known details of family life, Shakespeare's son Hamnet was buried at Stratford on August 11, 1596; his father was given a coat of arms on October 20, 1596; and he purchased New Place (a refurbished tourist attraction today) on May 4, 1597. The London playwright obviously had not severed connections with his birthplace, and he was reflecting his new affluence by being known as William Shakespeare of Stratford-upon-Avon, in the County of Warwick, Gentleman. His father was buried in Stratford on September 8, 1601; his mother, on September 9, 1608. His daughter Susanna married Dr. John Hall on June 5, 1607, and they had a child named Elizabeth. His other daughter, Judith, married Thomas Quiney on February 10, 1616, without special licence, during Lent and was thus excommunicated. Shakespeare revised his will on March 25, 1616, and was buried on April 25, 1616 (according to the parish register). A monument by Gerard Janssen was erected in the Holy Trinity chancel in 1623 but many, like Milton several years later, protested:

> What needs my *Shakespeare* for his honour'd Bones,
> The labour of an age in piled Stone, . . .
> Thou in our wonder and astonishment
> Hast built thy self a live-long Monument.

Shakespeare's Writings

Order of Appearance

Dating of Shakespeare's early plays, while based on inconclusive evidence, has tended to hover around the early 1590's. Almost certainly it is his chronicles of Henry the Sixth that Philip Henslowe, an important theatrical manager of the day, referred to in his diary as being performed during March-May, 1592. An allusion to these plays also occurs in Thomas Nashe's *Piers Penniless His Supplication to the Devil* (August, 1592). Greene's quotation about a tiger is a paraphrase of "O tiger's heart wrapt in a woman's hide" from *Henry VI*, Part III.

The first published work to come from Shakespeare's hand was *Venus and Adonis* (1593), a long stanzaic poem, dedicated to Henry

Wriothesley, Earl of Southampton. A year later *The Rape of Lucrece* appeared, also dedicated to Southampton. Perhaps poetry was pursued during these years because the London theaters were closed as a result of a virulent siege of plague. The *Sonnets*, published in 1609, may owe something to Southampton, who had become Shakespeare's patron. Perhaps some were written as early as the first few years of the 1590's. They were mentioned (along with a number of plays) in 1598 by Francis Meres in his *Palladis Tamia*, and sonnets 138 and 144 were printed without authority by William Jaggard in *The Passionate Pilgrim* (1599).

There is a record of a performance of *A Comedy of Errors* at Gray's Inn (one of the law colleges) on December 28, 1594, and, during early 1595, Shakespeare was paid, along with the famous actors Richard Burbage and William Kempe, for performances before the Queen by the Lord Chamberlain's Men, a theatrical company formed the year before. The company founded the Globe Theatre on the south side of the Thames in 1599 and became the King's Men when James ascended the throne. Records show frequent payments to the company through its general manager John Heminge. From 1595 through 1614 there are numerous references to real estate transactions and other legal matters, to many performances, and to various publications connected with Shakespeare.

Order of Publication

The first plays to be printed were *Titus Andronicus* around February, 1594, and the garbled versions of *Henry VI*, Parts II and III in 1594. (Some scholars, however, question whether the last two are versions of *Henry VI*, Parts II and III, and some dispute Shakespeare's authorship.) Thereafter *Richard III* appeared in 1597 and 1598; *Richard II*, in 1597 and twice in 1598; *Romeo and Juliet*, in 1597 (a pirated edition) and 1599, and many others. Some of the plays appear in individual editions, with or without Shakespeare's name on the title page, but eighteen are known only from their appearance in the first collected volume (the so-called First Folio) of 1623. The editors were Heminge and Henry Condell, another member of Shakespeare's company. *Pericles* was omitted from the First Folio although it had appeared in 1609, 1611, and 1619; it was added to the Third Folio in 1664.

There was reluctance to publish plays at this time for various reasons; many plays were carelessly written for fast production; collaboration was frequent; plays were not really considered *reading* matter; they were sometimes circulated in manuscript; and the theatrical company, not the author, owned the rights. Those plays given individual publication appeared in a quarto, so named from the size of the page. A single sheet of paper was folded twice to make four leaves (thus *quarto*) or eight pages; these four leaves constitute one signature (one section of a bound book). A page measures about 6¾ in. x 8½ in. On the other hand, a folio sheet is folded once to make two leaves or four pages; three sheets, or twelve pages, constitute a signature. The page is approximately 8½ in. x 13⅜ in.

Authorized publication occurred when a company disbanded, when money was needed but rights were to be retained, when a play failed or ran into licensing difficulties (thus, hopefully, the printed work would justify the play against the criticism), or when a play had been pirated. Authorized editions are called good quartos. Piratical publication might occur when the manuscript of a play had circulated privately, when a member of a company desired money for himself, or when a stenographer or memorizer took the play down in the theater (such a version was recognizable by inclusion of stage directions derived from an eyewitness, by garbled sections, etc.). Pirated editions are called bad quartos; there are at least five bad quartos of Shakespeare's plays.

Authenticity of Works

Usually thirty-seven plays are printed in modern collections of Shakespeare's works but some recent scholars have urged the addition of two more: *Edward III* and *Two Noble Kinsmen*. A case has also been advanced, unconvincingly, for a fragment of the play on Sir Thomas More. At times, six of the generally-accepted plays have been questioned: *Henry VI*, Parts I, II and III, *Timon of Athens*, *Pericles* and *Henry VIII*. The first four are usually accepted today (one hopes all question concerning *Timon* has finally ended), but if Shakespeare did not write these plays in their entirety, he certainly wrote parts of them. Of course, collaboration in those days was commonplace. Aside from the two long narrative poems already mentioned and the sonnets (Nos. 1-152, but not Nos. 153-154), Shakespeare's poetic output is uncertain. *The Passionate Pilgrim* (1599) contains only five authenticated poems (two sonnets and three verses from *Love's Labour's Lost*); *The Phoenix and the Turtle* (1601) may be his, but the authenticity of *A Lover's Complaint* (appended to the sonnets) is highly questionable.

Who Was Shakespeare?

At this point we might mention a problem that has plagued Shakespeare study for over a century: who was Shakespeare? Those who would like to make the author of the plays someone else — Francis Bacon or the Earl of Oxford or even Christopher Marlowe (dead long before most of the plays were written) — have used the lack of information of Shakespeare's early years and the confusion in the evidence we have been examining to advance their candidate. But the major arguments against Shakespeare show the source of these speculators' disbelief to be in classconscious snobbery and perhaps in a perverse adherence to minority opinion. The most common argument is that no one of Shakespeare's background, lack of education, and lack of aristocratic experience could know all that the author knew. But study will reveal that such information was readily available in various popular sources, that some of it lies in the literary sources used for the play, and that Shakespeare was probably not totally lacking in education or in social decorum. The more significant question of style and tone is not dealt with — nor could it successfully be raised. Bacon, for example, no matter how much we admire his mind and his writings, exhibits a writing style diametrically opposite to Shakespeare's, a style most unpoetic and often flat. The student would be wise not to waste time rehashing these unfounded theories. No such question was raised in the seventeenth or eighteenth centuries, and no serious student of the plays today doubts that Shakespeare *was* Shakespeare.

Shakespeare's Plays

Exact dates for Shakespeare's plays remain a source of debate among scholars. The following serve only as a general frame of reference.

	COMEDIES	TRAGEDIES	HISTORIES
1591			Henry VI, Part I
1592	Comedy of Errors		Henry VI, Part II
1592	Two Gentlemen of Verona		Henry VI, Part III
1593	Love's Labour's Lost	Titus Andronicus	Richard III
1594			King John
1595	Midsummer Night's Dream	Romeo and Juliet	Richard II
1596	Merchant of Venice		
1596	Taming of the Shrew		
1597			Henry IV, Part I
1598	Much Ado About Nothing		Henry IV, Part II
1599	As You Like It	Julius Caesar	
1599	Merry Wives of Windsor		Henry V
1601	Twelfth Night	Hamlet	
1602	Troilus and Cressida		
1602	All's Well That Ends Well		
1604	Measure for Measure	Othello	
1605		King Lear	
1606		Macbeth	
1607		Timon of Athens	
1607		Antony and Cleopatra	
1608	Pericles		
1609		Coriolanus	
1610	Cymbeline		
1611	Winter's Tale		
1611	Tempest		
1613			Henry VIII

Shakespeare's England

The world of Elizabethan and Jacobean England was a world of growth and change. The great increase in the middle class, and in the population as a whole, demanded a new economy and means of livelihood, a new instrument of government (one recognizing "rights" and changed class structure), a new social code and a broad base of entertainment. The invention of printing a century before had contributed to that broader base, but it was the theater that supplied the more immediate needs of the greatest numbers. The theater grew and along with it came less-educated, more money-conscious writers, who gave the people what they wanted: entertainment. But Shakespeare, having passed through a brief period of hack writing, proceeded to set down important ideas in memorable language throughout most of his career. His plays, particularly the later ones, have been analyzed by recent critics in terms of literary quality through their metaphor, verse-line, relationships with psychology and myth, and elaborate structure. Yet Shakespeare was a man of the stage, and the plays were written to be performed. Only this will fully account for the humor of a deadly serious play like *Hamlet* or the spectacle of a *Coriolanus*.

Life in London

During Shakespeare's early years there, London was a walled city of about 200,000, with seven gates providing access to the city from the east, north, and west. It was geographically small and crisscrossed by narrow little streets and lanes. The various wards each had a parish church that dominated the life of the close-knit community. To the south and outside were slums and the haunts of criminal types, and farther out were the agricultural lands and huge estates. As the population increased and the central area declined, the fashionable people of the city moved toward the west, where the palace of Westminster lay. Houses were generally rented out floor by floor and sometimes room by room. Slums were common within the city, too, though close to pleasant enough streets and squares. "Merrie Olde England" was not really clean, nor were its people, for in those days there were no sewers or drains except the gutter in the middle of the street, into which garbage would be emptied to be floated off by the rain to Fleet ditch or Moor ditch. Plague was particularly ravaging in 1592, 1593-94 (when the theaters were closed to avoid contamination) and 1603. Medical knowledge, of course, was slight; ills were "cured" by amputation, leeching, blood-letting and cathartics. The city was (and still is) dominated by St. Paul's Cathedral, around which booksellers clustered on Paternoster Row.

Religious Atmosphere

Of great significance for the times was religion. Under Elizabeth, a state church had developed; it was Protestant in nature and was called Anglican (or today, Episcopalian) but it had arisen from Henry VIII's break with the Pope and from a compromise with the Roman Catholics who had gained power under Mary Tudor.

The Church of England was headed by the Archbishop of Canter

7

bury, who was to be an increasingly important figure in the early part of the seventeenth century. There were also many schismatic groups, which generally desired further departures from Roman Catholicism. Calvinists were perhaps the most numerous and important of the Protestant groups. The Puritans, who were Calvinist, desired to "purify" the church of ritual and certain dogmas, but during the 1590's they were lampooned as extremists in dress and conduct.

Political Milieu

During Shakespeare's lifetime there were two monarchs: Elizabeth, 1558-1603, and James I, 1603-1625. Elizabeth was the daughter of Henry VIII and Anne Boleyn, his second wife, who was executed in 1536. After Henry's death, his son by his third wife, Jane Seymore (died in 1537), reigned as Edward VI. He was followed by Mary Tudor, daughter of Henry's first wife, Catherine of Aragon. Mary was a Roman Catholic, who tried to put down religious dissension by persecution of both Protestants and Catholics. Nor did her marriage to Philip II of Spain endear her to the people.

Elizabeth's reign was troubled by many offers of marriage, particularly from Spanish and French nobles — all Roman Catholic — and by the people's concern for an heir to the throne. English suitors generally cancelled one another out by intrigue or aggressiveness. One of the most prominent was the Earl of Essex, Robert Devereux, who fell in and out of favor; he apparently attempted to take over the reins of control, only to be captured, imprisoned and executed in February, 1601. One claimant to the throne was Mary of Scotland, a Roman Catholic and widow of Francis II of France. She was the second cousin of Elizabeth, tracing her claim through her grandmother, who was Henry VIII's sister. Finally, settlement came with Elizabeth's acceptance of Mary's son as heir apparent, though Mary was to be captured, tried and executed for treason in 1587. Mary had abdicated the throne of Scotland in 1567 in favor of her son, James VI. His ascent to the throne of England in 1603 as James I joined the two kingdoms for the first time, although Scotland during the seventeenth century often acted independently of England.

Contemporary Events

Political and religious problems were intermingled in the celebrated Gunpowder Plot. Angry over fines that were levied upon those not attending Church of England services — primarily Roman Catholics — and offended by difficulties over papal envoys, a group of Catholics plotted to blow up Parliament, and James with it, at its first session on November 5, 1605. A cache of gunpowder was stored in the cellar, guarded by various conspirators, among them Guy Fawkes. The plot was discovered before it could be carried out and Fawkes, on duty at the time, was apprehended. The execution of the plotters and the triumph of the anti-Papists led in succeeding years to celebrations in the streets and the hanging of Fawkes in effigy.

Among the most noteworthy public events during these times were the wars with the Spanish, which included the defeat of the Spanish Armada in 1588, the battle in the Lowlands in 1590-1594, the expedition to Cadiz under Essex in 1596 and the expedition to the Azores (the Islands Expedition), also under Essex, in 1597. With trading companies especially set up for colonization and exploitation, travel excited the imagination of the people: here was a new way of life, here were new customs brought back by the sailors and merchants, here was a new dream world to explore.

In all, the years from around 1590 to 1601 were trying ones for English people, relieved only by the news from abroad, the new affluence and the hope for the future under James. Writers of the period frequently reflect, however, the disillusionment and sadness of those difficult times.

The Elizabethan Theater

Appearance

The Elizabethan playhouse developed from the medieval inn with its rooms grouped around a courtyard into which a stage was built. This pattern was used in The Theatre, built by James Burbage in 1576: a square frame building (later round or octagonal) with a square yard, three tiers of galleries, each jutting out over the one below, and a stage extending into the middle of the yard, where people stood or sat on improvised seats. There was no cover over the yard or stage and lighting was therefore natural. Thus performances were what we might consider late matinees or early evening performances; in summer, daylight continues in London until around ten o'clock.

Other theaters were constructed during the ensuing years: The Curtain in 1577, The Rose in 1587 (on Bankside), The Swan in 1595 (also Bankside) and Shakespeare's playhouse, The Globe, in 1599 (not far from The Rose). There is still some question about the exact dimensions of this house, but it seems to have been octagonal, each side measuring about 36 feet, with an over-all diameter of 84 feet. It was about 33 feet to the eaves, and the yard was 56 feet in diameter. Three sides were used for backstage and to serve the needs of the players. There was no curtain or proscenium, hence the spectators became part of the action. Obviously, the actors' asides and soliloquies were effective under these conditions.

There was no real scenery and there were only a few major props; thus the lines of the play had to reveal locations and movement, changes in time or place, etc. In this way, too, it was easier to establish a nonrealistic setting, for all settings were created in words. On either side of the stage were doors, within the flooring were trapdoors (for entrances of ghosts, etc.), and behind the main stage was the inner stage or recess. Here, indoor scenes (such as a court or a bedchamber) were played, and some props could be used because the inner stage was usually concealed by a curtain when not in use. It might also have served to hide someone behind the ever-present arras, like Polonius in *Hamlet*. The "chamber" was on the second level, with windows and a balcony. On the third level was another chamber, primarily for musicians.

Actors

An acting company such as the Lord Chamberlain's Men was a fellowship of ten to fifteen sharers with some ten to twelve extras, three or four boys (often to play women's roles) who might become full sharers, and stagehands. There were rival companies, each with its leading dramatist and leading tragic actor and clown. The Lord Admiral's Men, organized in 1594, boasted Ben Jonson and the tragedian Edward Alleyn. Some of the rivalry of this War of the Theaters is reflected in the speeches of Hamlet, who also comments on the ascendancy and unwarranted popularity of the children's companies (like the Children of Blackfriars) in the late 1590's.

The company dramatist, of course, had to think in terms of the members of his company as he wrote his play. He had to make use of the physical features and peculiar talents of the actors, making sure, besides, that there was a role for each member. The fact that women's parts were taken by boys imposed obvious limitations on the range of action. Accordingly, we often find women characters impersonating men; for example, Robert Goffe played Portia in *The Merchant of Venice*, and Portia impersonates a male lawyer in the important trial scene. Goffe also played Juliet, and Anne in *Richard III*, and Oberon in *Midsummer Night's Dream*. The influence of an actor on the playwright can be seen, on the one hand, by noting the "humor" characters portrayed so competently by Thomas Pope, who was a choleric Mercutio in *Romeo*, a melancholic Jaques in *As You Like It*, and a sanguinary Falstaff in *Henry IV*, Part I; and by comparing, on the other hand, the clown Bottom in *Midsummer Night's Dream*, played in a frolicsome manner by William Kempe, with the clown Feste in *Twelfth Night*, sung and danced by Robert Armin. Obviously, too, if a certain kind of character was not available within the company, then that kind of character could not be written into the play. The approach was decidedly different from ours today, where the play almost always comes first and the casting of roles second. The plays were performed in a repertory system, with a different play each afternoon. The average life of a play was about ten performances.

History of the Drama

English drama goes back to native forms developed from playlets presented at Church holidays. Mystery plays dealt with biblical stories such as the Nativity or the Passion, and miracle plays usually depicted the lives of saints. The merchant and craft guilds that came to own and produce the cycles of plays were the forerunners of the theatrical companies of Shakespeare's time. The kind of production these cycles received, either as moving pageants in the streets or as staged shows in a churchyard, influenced the late sixteenth-century production of a secular play: there was an intimacy with the audience and there was a great reliance on words rather than setting and props. Similar involvement with the stage action is experienced by audiences of the arena theater of today.

The morality play, the next form to develop, was an allegory of the spiritual conflict between good and evil in the soul of man. The *dramatis personae* were abstract virtues and vices, with at least one man representing Mankind (or Everyman, as the most popular of these plays was titled). Some modern critics see *Othello* as a kind of morality play in which the soul of Othello is vied for by the aggressively evil Iago (as a kind of Satanic figure) and passively good Desdemona (as a personification of Christian faith in all men). The Tudor interlude — a short, witty, visual play — may have influenced the subplot of the Elizabethan play with its low-life and jesting and visual tricks. In mid-sixteenth century appeared the earliest known English comedies, Nicholas Udall's *Ralph Roister Doister* and *Gammer Gurton's Needle* (of uncertain authorship). Both show the influence of the Roman comic playwright Plautus. Shakespeare's *Comedy of Errors*, performed in the 1590's, was an adaptation of Plautus' *Menaechmi*, both plays featuring twins and an involved story of confused identities. The influence of the Roman tragedian Seneca can be traced from Thomas Norton and Thomas Sackville in *Gorboduc* to *Hamlet*. Senecan tragedy is a tragedy of revenge, characterized by many deaths, much blood-letting, ghosts, feigned madness and the motif of a death for a death.

Shakespeare's Artistry

Plots

Generally, a Shakespearean play has two plots: a main plot and a subplot. The subplot reflects the main plot and is often concerned with inferior characters. Two contrasting examples will suffice: Lear and his daughters furnish the characters for the main plot of filial love and ingratitude, whereas Gloucester and his sons enact the same theme in the subplot; Lear and Gloucester both learn that outward signs of love may be false. In *Midsummer Night's Dream*, the town workmen (Quince, Bottom *et al.*) put on a tragic play in such a hilarious way that it turns the subject of the play — love so strong that the hero will kill himself if his loved one dies first — into farce, but this in the main plot is the "serious" plight of the four mixed-up lovers. In both examples Shakespeare has reinforced his points by subplots dealing with the same subject as the main plot.

Sources

The plots of the Elizabethan plays were usually adapted from other sources. "Originality" was not the sought quality; a kind of variation on a theme was. It was felt that one could better evaluate the playwright's worth by seeing what he did with a familiar tale. What he stressed, how he stressed it, how he restructured the familiar elements — these were the important matters. Shakespeare closely followed Sir Thomas North's very popular translation of Plutarch's *Life of Marcus Antonius*, for example, in writing *Antony and Cleopatra*; and he modified Robert Greene's *Pandosto* and combined it with the Pygmalion myth in *The Winter's Tale*, while drawing the character of Autolycus from certain pamphlets written by Greene. The only plays for which sources have not been clearly determined are *Love's Labour's Lost* (probably based on contemporary events) and *The Tempest* (possibly based on some shipwreck account from travellers to the New World).

Verse and Prose

There is a mixture of verse and prose in the plays, partially because plays fully in verse were out of fashion. Greater variety could thus be achieved and character or atmosphere could be more precisely delineated. Elevated passages, philosophically significant ideas, speeches by men of high rank are in verse, but comic and light parts, speeches including dialect or broken English, and scenes that move more rapidly or simply give mundane information are in prose. The poetry is almost always blank verse (iambic pentameter lines without rhyme). Rhyme is used, however (particularly the couplet), to mark the close of scenes or an important action. Rhyme also serves as a cue for the entrance of another actor or some off-stage business, to point to a change of mood or thought, as a forceful opening after a passage of prose, to convey excitement or passion or sentimentality and to distinguish characters.

Shakespeare's plays may be divided into three general categories, though some plays are not readily classified and further subdivisions may be suggested within a category.

The History Play

The history play, or chronicle, may tend to tragedy, like *Richard II*, or to comedy, like *Henry IV*, Part I. It is a chronicle of some royal personage, often altered for dramatic purposes, even to the point of falsification of the facts. Its popularity may have resulted from the rising of nationalism of the English, nurtured by their successes against the Spanish, their developing trade and colonization, and their rising prestige as a world power. The chronicle was considered a political guide, like the popular *Mirror for Magistrates*, a collection of writings showing what happens when an important leader falls through some error in his ways, his thinking or his personality. Thus the history play counseled the right path by negative, if not positive, means. Accordingly, it is difficult to call *Richard II* a tragedy, since Richard was wrong and his wrongness harmed his people. The political philosophy of Shakespeare's day seemed to favor the view that all usurpation was bad and should be corrected, but not by further usurpation. When that original usurpation had been established, through an heir's ascension to the throne, it was to be accepted. Then any rebellion against the "true" king would be a rebellion against God.

Tragedy

Tragedy in simple terms meant that the protagonist died. Certain concepts drawn from Aristotle's *Poetics* require a tragic hero of high standing, who must oppose some conflicting force, either external or internal. The tragic hero should be dominated by a *hamartia* (a so-called tragic flaw, but really an *excess* of some character trait, e.g., pride, or *hubris*), and it is this *hamartia* that leads to his downfall and, because of his status, to the downfall of others. The action presented in the tragedy must be recognizable to the audience as real and potential: through seeing it enacted, the audience has its passion (primarily suffering) raised, and the conclusion of the action thus brings release from that passion (*catharsis*). A more meaningful way of looking at tragedy in the Elizabethan theater, however, is to see it as that which occurs when essential good (like Hamlet) is wasted (through disaster or death) in the process of driving out evil (such as Claudius represents).

Comedy

Comedy in simple terms meant that the play ended happily for the protagonists. Sometimes the comedy depends on exaggerations of man's eccentricities — comedy of humors; sometimes the comedy is romantic and far-fetched. The romantic comedy was usually based on a mix-up in events or confused identity of characters, particularly by disguise. It moved toward tragedy in that an important person might die and the mix-up might never be unraveled; but in the nick of time something happens or someone appears (sometimes illogically or unexpectedly) and saves the day. It reflects the structure of myth by moving from happiness to despair to resurrection. *The Winter's Tale* is a perfect example of this, for the happiness of the first part is banished with Hermione's exile and Perdita's abandonment; tragedy is near when the lost baby, Perdita, cannot be found and Hermione is presumed dead, but Perdita reappears, as does Hermione, a statue that suddenly comes to life. Lost identities are established and confusions disappear but the mythic-comic nature of the play is seen in the reuniting of the mother, Hermione, a kind of Ceres, with her daughter, Perdita, a kind of Prosperina. Spring returns, summer will bring the harvest, and the winter of the tale is left behind — for a little while.

What is it, then, that makes Shakespeare's art so great? Perhaps we see in it a whole spectrum of humanity, treated impersonally, but with kindness and understanding. We seldom meet in Shakespeare a weeping philosopher: he may criticize, but he criticizes both sides. After he has done so, he gives the impression of saying, Well, that's the way life is; people will always be like that — don't get upset about it. This is probably the key to the Duke's behavior in *Measure for Measure* — a most unbitter comedy despite former labels. Only in *Hamlet* does Shakespeare not seem to fit this statement; it is the one play that Shakespeare, the person, enters.

As we grow older and our range of experience widens, so, too, does Shakespeare's range seem to expand. Perhaps this lies in the ambiguities of his own materials, which allow for numerous individual readings. We meet our own experiences — and they are ours alone, we think — expressed in phrases that we thought our own or of our own discovery. What makes Shakespeare's art so great, then, is his ability to say so much to so many people in such memorable language: he is himself "the show and gaze o' the time."

JULIUS CAESAR

Historical Background to the Play

When Rome was founded in 753 B.C. as a city-state, the king (chief priest, judge, and supreme war lord) maintained an advisory council of heads of leading families, the Senate. The people (*populus*), composed of plebians and clients, were grouped by kinships into *curiae*, and for military service into *centuriae* (nominal hundreds). The richer citizenry, those who owned horses, were *equites* (knights), and served as cavalry; the poorer were infantry troops. Those without property could not bear arms. Assemblies of the people were known as *comitia*. Voting was done by groups; a majority in each curia or centuria decided the group wishes; a majority of groups decided the issues.

The Republic

Toward the end of the sixth century B.C., patricians expelled the tyrant, Tarquinius Superbus, and the monarchy became a republic. This change created a serious problem: how to organize and control the army so that civil liberties would not be violated and yet, at the same time, safeguard the new republic against aggression. The patricians immediately usurped kingly power and vested this in two *praetors* (leaders), later termed *consuls*, who were elected yearly by the Assembly of the people. It was the consuls, however, who selected new members of the Senate for life-long tenure and, since the consuls were selected from the senatorial families, patrician control was assured. The system of government had a serious flaw: there was no police force within Rome (such as the king's bodyguard, who would have functioned in this capacity) and none was established because of fear of despotism. This left the patrician ruling group vulnerable to plebian struggles during the period from 494 to 287 B.C.

Although the plebians were theoretically the source of power, actually they were deprived of this political advantage by the tight clique of senatorial rulers. To protect themselves from social and economic abuses, they organized themselves into a protective body which had its own assembly (*concilia plebis*) and appointed its own officers, the tribunes (*tribuni plebis*), to secure their rights. This set-up was, in effect, secession within the state, and at least five such secessions occurred during the aforementioned period.

At first this counter-organization within the government (*concilium plebis* and *tribunes*) could not pass laws because it did not represent the whole of the people, but by 287 B.C. plebian resolutions (*plebicita*) were eventually given legal status, and plebians won the right of admission to offices and, eventually, to the Senate. Like the consuls, the tribunes were elected yearly. Not only could they initiate laws, but they could also veto consul proposals and those of their colleagues as well. However, this form of government did not constitute a democracy. To all intents and purposes it was nothing more

15

than a dual organization of governmental bodies acting simultaneously but almost independently of each other.

To add to the existing evils, in 366 B.C. the office of *Praetor* (in addition to consuls) was established to supervise the judiciary in Rome; then others were added to provide governors for the overseas provinces, and these praetors had full consular powers. To retain those consuls who commanded besieging armies (in cases where the siege lasted for more than a year), *proconsuls* were appointed by the Assembly. This means of increasing officers with *imperium* (absolute dominion) without altering the number of consuls in Rome (or their tenure) created a mad scramble for power.

The Rise of the Empire

As Rome extended her dominion to Sicily, Italy, Greece, the east and west Mediterranean areas, Spain, Gaul, Britain and Africa, plebian rights were so subordinated to the wartime rights of the Assembly that the plebians lost their power by 148 B.C.

The conquests rapidly changed the economic situation in Rome. Ancient wars were profitable. The Romans, who were never industrially inclined, needed gold; and the simplest way to solve the growing demands for money and revenue was by plunder. Between 200 and 167 B.C. the estimated yield was 31,000 pounds of gold, 669,000 pounds of silver, and total tribute of 5,000,000 pounds. The second precious commodity of war was manpower: prisoners became valuable assets in the slave trade, and slave breeding developed into a thriving business.

The picture soon changed: the falling prices for slaves on a glutted market made it possible for people of moderate means to buy at least ten, and the wealthy to own two hundred or more, where once only a nobleman could afford a pair of servitors. This unprecedented influx of slaves had two lasting effects on the social structure: Roman culture took on Hellenic aspects; the pure Latin stock was interfused with that of the enslaved peoples and eventually the new blood strains were absorbed into the citizenry of Rome.

The wars, of course, were profitable only to the speculators. Agriculture was disrupted; landowners who had not fallen in battle returned after lengthy service to mortgaged or lost farms, only to find that crops from the conquered areas were cheaper than their own produce. Shrewd profiteers could obtain credit easily and buy land and slaves for a pittance. Since senators were forbidden to engage in commerce, army contractors were drawn from the knights. These men reaped such fabulous profits out of war that soon they controlled most of the arable land because slave labor was cheap and not subject to army conscription. The dispossessed small farmers could only flock to Rome.

Other inequalities followed in the wake of expansion. The owners of large estates (*latifundia*) formed financial syndicates in order to collect provincial revenues for the Republic (Rome had no official tax collectors), and although governors were not permitted to hold shares in these syndicates, many did, for they could protect themselves from extortion charges by bribing jurors. As the senators joined the syndicates in increasing numbers, these "banking houses" became strong enough to ruin even the most powerful of those who advocated reforms.

The new proletariat of Rome (the ousted farmers) soon learned to sell their votes in magisterial elections at good prices. The politically ambitious, to gain the support of the voters, had to finance lavish campaign spectacles and soon fell prey to the bankers. The bankers pursued their corrupt strangle hold on the public, patrician and plebian alike. Money became king in the materialistic society of Rome. This was precisely the state of affairs in Rome when Julius Caesar made his bid for power.

Caesar and Roman Politics

Throughout a long history of civil dissension, tyrants had been deposed only to be replaced by others even more corrupt. Caesar, by contrast, was a welcome relief.

L. Cornelius Sulla, the strong consul who had stabilized chaotic conditions in Rome and restored order in the provinces, resigned his position as dictator, confident that the minor political reforms that he had instituted would assure the restoration of power to the Senate. When he died in 78 B.C., trouble, instigated by the counter-revolutionary policies of M. Aemilius Lepidus, one of the consuls, broke out in Northern Etruria. Pompey, who had been "retired" by Sulla for a tactless bid for power, was called to march against Lepidus. Pompey routed Lepidus and became the uncrowned emperor of the East.

Caesar, recognizing the possibilities, joined in the First Triumvirate in 60 B.C. with Gnaeus Pompey and Marcus Crassus. The alliance seemed mutually complementary: Pompey, the brilliant strategist and administrator, lacked diplomacy; Caesar, the lucky strategist, was an astute politician and statesman; Crassus, endowed with a great fortune, could supply funds that Caesar seldom had. In a campaign against the Parthians in 53 B.C., Crassus was conveniently eliminated by his own men when he tried to halt their panicked rout after water conduits had been flooded with sea water. The rivalry between the two remaining triumvirs was temporarily abated by Caesar's victories in Italy in 49 B.C., for which he was appointed dictator and consul. As one of the Popular Party, he was also made a tribune for life. At Pharsalus (Greece) the following year, he defeated Pompey, but could not establish a firm hold until he had followed through with campaigns in Egypt, Tunis, and Spain. In these, he crushed the remaining Pompey adherents, including his rival's two sons. Although, technically, the position of dictatorship was a temporary bestowal of supreme command for a limited period of national danger, Caesar was made dictator for life. Not content with power alone, Caesar made overtures, with the aid of the Popular Party (though a patrician, Caesar had always been affiliated with the *Popularis*), for supreme honor. His assassination in 44 B.C. touched off the series of events related in *The Tragedy of Julius Caesar*.

Shakespeare's Source

With the advent of the printing press, one of the first ancient classics to attain widespread popularity during the Renaissance was the *Parallel Lives of Greeks and Romans* by Plutarch of Chaeronea (46-120 A.D.). First printed in Latin in Rome (1470), it was translated by Bishop Jacques Amyot into French in 1559, and from the French into English by Sir Thomas North as the *Lives of the Noble Grecians and Romans*. North's first English edition appeared in 1579 (a volume of 1,175 pages detailing the lives of fifty men), a second edition was released in 1595, and a third was issued in 1630 and reprinted in 1612. A costly volume, this book was a bestseller because of the Renaissance interest in ancient classics and because Plutarch, in setting forth exceptionally perceptive character analyses of famous ancients, impartially described these men, their times, and their influence as molders of history. Informed Elizabethans, who saw in the ancient Roman civil wars parallels to their own Wars of the Roses, were generally quite familiar with the *Lives*.

It was natural that Shakespeare should have been inspired by this source and have used it extensively in *Julius Caesar* (and in his other Roman plays). The dramatist based incidents and even dialogue on North's account of the lives of Caesar, Brutus, and Marcus Antonius, frequently combining versions of all three accounts and sometimes deviating from the materials and time sequence so as to enhance the dramatic quality of his work (*eg.* the actual reason for the omission of Marullus and Flavius, for the version of Portia's suicide, and for the deliberate blurring of the lapse in time between certain incidents). As an Elizabethan, influenced by the attitudes of his times, Shakespeare glossed over certain political implications and left provocative or controversial points to the interpretation of the audience, for while the knowledgeable among them understood the inferences and could draw their own conclusions, the average man could still enjoy the dramatic spectacle of an ancient tragedy.

The Plutarchan Version

Plutarch, as an impartial historian, probed deeply into the nature of political power and the effects that such power could have on men and the course of history. In fact, *Julius Caesar* can be regarded not only as a tragedy, but as a political "problem play" in which each character presents his own approach to the problem of power.

Caesar, fresh from victories in Gaul, pursued a badly demoralized Pompey to Brundusium, from whence he fled to Egypt and his death. Chosen Consul for the fourth time after his defeat of Pompey's sons in Spain (previous to that he had conquered Egypt), Caesar was not content with that position but had to reach for perpetual dictatorship, which was granted to him. Once having established himself in the confidence of Rome, by means of personal charm, leadership, and clemency to former opponents (Cassius and Brutus were pardoned and made Praetors), Caesar reached for kingship.

Backed by staunch supporters and a loyal army, Caesar was well on the way to that goal. Much as the populace admired Caesar, it was wary about offering him the coveted position. Cicero, although he was the first to propose honors for Caesar, withdrew his support when he saw other members of the Senate outdoing each other in vying for Caesar's favor. The offenses that the tribunes Marullus and Flavius committed were the removing of diadems from statues of Caesar and the imprisoning of those who had prematurely hailed Caesar as king.

Marcus Brutus had a tradition of nobility and noble conduct to live up to. Descended from the Junius Brutus who had vanquished the Tarquin tyrants, he was nephew (through his mother, Servilia) to Marcus Cato, the philosopher, and married to Cato's daughter, Portia. Despite a close relationship with Caesar (Brutus was born to Servilia during a time when her romance with Caesar was at its peak, and Caesar persuaded himself that he had sired Brutus), Brutus sided with Pompey. This did not diminish Caesar's love for Brutus, for the conqueror gave orders that the young man was to be protected during the heat of battle, and when Brutus and Cassius contended for the chief Praetorship, Caesar awarded the position to Brutus although Cassius had seniority and was the abler soldier. This decision made Cassius an implacable foe of Caesar and caused a rift between Brutus and Cassius. According to Plutarch, it was friends who threw in the inflammatory bills, and friends who urged Cassius to patch up the quarrel, for none would join Cassius in the conspiracy unless Brutus could be induced to take part. Brutus finally consented and according to the assassination account, "so many swords and daggers lighting upon one body, one of them hurt another, and among them Brutus caught a blow on his hand." Following the assassination, the Senate, having regained its composure, decided the next morning to accept the motion of Antonius, Plancus and Cicero "to pardon and forget all that was past" in the interest of peace, but Antonius' funeral oration for Caesar so enraged the citizenry that Brutus and Cassius had to flee from Rome.

Here, it would be well to digress in order to briefly review the backgrounds of Marcus Antonius and Octavius Caesar (later to become Augustus Caesar). It was during the latter's reign that the Roman Empire reached its zenith.

Marcus Antonius sought to confirm by action, manner and apparel the family tradition that the Antonii were descended from Anton, son of Hercules. Antony, because of eloquent oratory and his generosity with funds that Caesar supplied, was chosen Tribune and later Augur. When Caesar left for Spain he left Lepidus (then Praetor) as Governor of Rome and Antonius (then Tribune) in charge of the troops and Italy. Antonius endeared himself to the troops by his liberality and ability to fraternize, but offended others by injustice and improper behavior. Nevertheless, Caesar recognized his subordinate's military prowess and as Caesar went up the ladder, Antonius followed. In time, however, Antonius' excesses in private and public life became so offensive that Caesar chose Lepidus over Antonius as his second. Marriage to a clever and cultured woman, Fulvia (widow of Clodius), somewhat subdued the flamboyant Antonius. After Caesar's death, Antonius gained the confidence of Calphurnia, who advanced him four thousand talents and turned over Caesar's books and writings to him. Thus, as Consul, he ruled Rome until Octavius Caesar appeared.

Octavius Caesar, Julius' legal heir (grandson of his sister) was a student in Apollonia when the assassination occurred. Receiving news of Caesar's death, he adopted his benefactor's name and hurried back to Rome. Antonius tried to dissuade the young Octavius (he was then only twenty) from administering the bequests that Caesar had made (he had left seventy-five drachmas to every citizen of Rome and his gardens and arbors on the Tiber to the public), but Octavius appealed to Cicero for help. When Antonius realized that Octavius was gathering support among his uncle's troops, he decided upon a closer alliance with the young heir. Cicero, meanwhile, had forced Antonius out of Italy, and Antonius endured lean times until he could return to Italy with sufficient troops to impress Octavius.

Brutus, during this period of a divided Rome, had left Italy for Athens, where he was favorably received. There, under guise of pursuing further studies, he secretly prepared for war in Asia and enlisted the aid of young compatriots. Octavius had antagonized the Senate by keeping a huge standing army, and the Senate again turned to Brutus and appointed him governor of certain provinces. This move caused Octavius to ally himself with Antonius. Octavius' next move was to force the Senate to appoint him Consul and, as Consul, he appointed judges to accuse and condemn Brutus and Cassius on the grounds of regicide. A new triumvirate composed of Octavius, Antonius and Lepidus divided the provinces between themselves and set up the proscription lists that condemned two hundred noble Romans to death (another account mentions three hundred), among them Cicero. (Brutus claimed that he was more ashamed of the cause of Cicero's death than sorry for his death, and that conditions in Rome were due not so much to the power of tyranny as to the cowardliness of the Romans who countenanced such abuses.) Antonius, to further bind Octavius to him, arranged for the young heir's marriage to Fulvia's daughter, Claudia. The new triumvirate soon became hateful to the Romans, and Octavius, realizing that no amount of money would cover Antonius' extravagances, divided the money between them, and both decided to wage war on Brutus and Cassius, leaving the city of Rome in charge of Lepidus.

Brutus, who was now in Asia gathering ships for his considerable army, sent word to Cassius, who was then in Syria preparing to go on to Egypt, that Rome needed them; this was not the time for personal conquest. Deferring to Cassius' age and weakened state of health, Brutus met Cassius at Smyrna. Plutarch here describes Cassius as choleric and cruel, a man who ruled men by fear rather than respect, and Brutus as one who was so noble in thought and deportment that even Antonius never doubted Brutus' motive for the slaying of Caesar. It was at this meeting that Brutus appealed to Cassius for funds and, although the latter's friends deplored his generosity, Cassius gave him money. Cassius then took the city of Rhodes before joining Brutus at Sardis.

The accounts of the Battle of Philippi and the tragic deaths (allowing for Shakespeare's confusion of the time element and Plutarch's lengthier and more comprehensive detailing) are essentially the same, except for the following details. Brutus' ashes were sent back to his mother, Servilia. Portia, determined to kill herself (although her parents and friends kept careful watch to prevent her) took hot coals into her mouth and kept her mouth closed so that she choked herself. There is also mention of a letter by Brutus complaining of the negligence of his friends in allowing Portia, a sick woman, to kill herself.

The Elizabethan Political Atmosphere

The Elizabethan concept of society and government was that of a fixed order in which every rank had its special functions, responsibilities and rights. Such a complex organization could not be violated with impunity; to disturb the natural order of things by violent means was to start a chain-reaction which could only conclude with the chaos and tragedy of civil war. The king was the God-given sovereign of an ordered society, duly anointed by the head of the Anglican Church, and as such he was sacred. It is, therefore, understandable that the Tudor monarchs, from Henry VII through Elizabeth I, encouraged this concept and its accompanying principle of *passive obedience* to the sovereign as one sent by God to rule the state. If the royal power were tyrannical and unjust, that was God's will; the people were to pray for God to soften the king's heart and to lead him into better ways, but under no conditions were the people to take matters into their own hands, or to attempt to delegate to another what God had given one man.

The English knew from past experience what civil strife could do and so they readily supported the doctrine of passive obedience. The Wars of the Roses (between the Houses of York and Lancaster) had lasted through almost the third quarter of the fifteenth century. Although Henry VII, born a Tudor, claimed that the two warring families were united in himself by his marriage to Elizabeth of York, he was nevertheless plagued by rebel activities, and several times during his reign he had to raise armies to put down the discontented peasantry or Yorkists. Throughout the sixteenth century, during the reigns of Henry VIII, Edward, Mary and Elizabeth, dangerous conspiracies and insurrections continued. Elizabeth's long rule (1558-1603) not only suffered the reverberations of internal instability, but the added threat that invasion by Spain might cause another civil war.

To the Elizabethans, the threats of political assassination and civil war were ever imminent, and it is natural that Shakespeare viewed these menaces with repugnance and, like other Elizabethans, accepted passive obedience as the means by which a society functioned effectively. In *Julius Caesar*, the Elizabethans considered Brutus' part in the assassination as the fatal error of a misguided man who plunged his country into civil strife. Since he and his co-conspirator were punished for their conduct, the play was a moral object lesson and Shakespeare in no way offended the sensibilities of his absolute monarch, nor of her subjects.

Plot Summary

Rome is divided by political strife as Caesar makes his triumphant entry into the city in 44 B.C. on the Feast of Lupercal (February 15), following his defeat of Pompey's sons. The ignorant, emotional populace acts favorably toward the strongman image built up by Caesar. The free-born patricians, on the other hand, jealous of the people's republican rights and privileges, are bitterly opposed to rule by one man. Fearing Caesar's ambitions, the tribunes Marullus and Flavius criticize Caesar before the assembled crowds and strip the statues of his trophies.

While attending the traditional foot race given on this holiday, Caesar is warned by a soothsayer to "Beware the Ides of March." Caesar arrogantly dismisses this warning as he departs for the race course, leaving Caesar's friend Brutus with the wily Cassius, who carefully plays upon Brutus' fears of Caesar's ambition in an attempt to enlist Brutus in the conspiracy against Caesar.

As Caesar, obviously disturbed, returns with his entourage, he voices his distrust of Cassius to Mark Antony and again departs. Brutus and Cassius detain Casca, from whom they learn that Caesar was thrice offered the crown, had thrice rejected it (each time more reluctantly), and then had been seized by an epileptic fit when the crowd cheered his refusals.

A month later (the eve of the Ides of March) Cicero and Casca meet during a storm. Casca relates a series of disturbing, unnatural events. When Cicero leaves, Cassius joins the badly shaken Casca and interprets the unnatural happenings as portents of what will happen to Rome if Caesar's ambitions are realized. Cinna joins the two and receives instructions from Cassius to throw another inflammatory letter into Brutus' window (to draw the hesitant Brutus into the conspiracy). The three depart after making arrangements to meet later at Pompey's Porch where Decius Brutus, Trebonius, and Metellus Cimber await them. Brutus is drawn into the conspiracy that night and leaves in the morning with Caius Ligarius to join the other conspirators in their prearranged plan to accompany Caesar to the Capitol.

Calphurnia, Caesar's wife, has had a disturbing dream and begs Caesar to remain at home. Decius Brutus, however, convinces Caesar that Calphurnia has misinterpreted her dream, that it is really a good omen. Caesar leaves for the Capitol with Mark Antony, the senator Publius, and all of the conspirators except Cassius. On the way, Caesar refuses to listen to the warnings of Artemidorus and a soothsayer, and once in the Capitol, Mark

Antony's attention is diverted by Trebonius while the bloody assassination is carried out according to plan.

Mark Antony, who had fled the scene of the stabbing, returns to the Capitol and, feigning approval of the assassination, asks for permission to make the funeral oration for Caesar. Brutus complies despite Cassius' objections. In the market place Brutus makes a simple speech to the people. Antony beginning cautiously, slowly swings the crowd to his side with subtle references to Caesar's past virtues, his generous bequests, and then turns the crowd into a rioting mob crying for vengeance. Antony then joins Octavius Caesar and Lepidus at Caesar's house, and together the new triumvirate plan to oppose the military threat of Brutus and Cassius.

On the plains of Philippi the two opposing factions meet for battle. Much has gone on in the meantime: both factions have been plagued by rivalry and dissension among the leaders; Portia (the wife of Brutus) has committed suicide, and one hundred senators have been put to death by the new triumvirs. But most important, Brutus has overridden Cassius' suggestion that they wait for the enemy to come to them on the heights of Sardis and has decided, instead, that they go down to meet the enemy at Philippi. Brutus and Cassius make their farewell with the premonition that they may never meet again.

At Philippi, Brutus sends Messala to Cassius with an urgent plea for him to move at once in a decisive thrust at Octavius' forces. Cassius cannot comply; his men have been forced into retreat by Antony's encircling troops because Brutus' men, having permaturely driven back Octavius' forces, are too busily engaged in looting to come to the aid of their allies. The confusion is such that Cassius cannot distinguish friend from foe. Mistakenly assuming that his messenger, Titinius, has fallen into the hands of the enemy, and that the enemy has won, Cassius asks Pindarus to stab him. Returning, Titinius enters with Messala, discovers Cassius' body, and kills himself. Messala reports the tragedy to Brutus and, together with Cato, Strato, Volumnius and Lucilius, they pay a sad farewell and leave for the encounter with the enemy.

As Brutus spurs his men on, Lucilius is captured by Antony's soldiers and mistaken for Brutus until Antony recognizes him. Brutus, meanwhile, rests with a few friends and the remnants of his army as he pleads with his friends, Clitus, Dardanius and Volumnius to help him commit suicide. Strato finally consents to hold the sword while Brutus falls upon it. Antony, Octavius, Messala and Lucilius enter with other soldiers to find Strato with the body of Brutus. It is Antony who delivers the eulogy describing Brutus as "the noblest Roman of them all," and Octavius who orders an honored burial for the self-slain foe before they leave to share the "glories of this happy day."

Chronology of the Play

	In Shakespeare (6 days with intervals)	History (3 years)
Day 1	Act I, Scenes 1 and 2 — Caesar's triumph and the Lupercal.	Caesar's triumph for his victory at Munda (B.C. 45, Oct.) Festival of Lupercal (B.C. 44, Feb. 15)
Interval	Unspecified	1 month, during which Caesar prepares for expedition into Illyricum and Parthia
Day 2	Act I, Sc. 2 — Night time	
Day 3	Acts II and III — Before dawn Act II, Sc. 1 — 8:00 a.m. Act II, Sc. 2 — 9:00 a.m.	Assassination of Caesar (Ides of March — B.C. 44, March 15)
Interval	Unspecified	Interval of more than 7 months Brutus in Macedonia, Cassius in Syria
Day 4	Act IV, Sc. 1	Three-day conference of the triumvirate at Bononia (B.C. 43, Oct.)
Interval	Unspecified	Interval of about 3 months. The Proscription is proclaimed; Cicero and others put to death.
Day 5	Act IV, Scenes 2 and 3	Antony and Octavius prepare for battle at their quarters in Amphipolis.
Day 6	Act V — The two battles at Philippi described as one.	Battle of Phillipi — The second battle 20 days after the first. (B.C. 42, Oct.)

Summaries and Commentaries
by Act and Scene

ACT I · SCENE I

Summary

Julius Caesar is celebrating a "triumph" in Rome for the defeat of Pompey's sons after Pompey's death. It is the end of one of the terrible destructive civil wars that tore the Roman world apart during this period. Up to this time it has not been the custom to celebrate "triumphs" (triumphal processions through the city) over any defeated persons but foreigners, and certainly not over Roman fellow-citizens. Hence, the bitterness of those who are not in sympathy with Caesar.

Flavius and Marullus enter. They are two tribunes of the people, magistrates with very considerable powers and who are traditionally and legally sacred. They are sending home a number of humble craftsmen whose only offence is that they have taken a holiday from their occupations to be spectators at this triumphal procession of Caesar's. (The Roman citizen of the period had a much greater delight in all kinds of public pageantry than the average citizen of today.) These tribunes are really supposed to be protectors of the rights of the common people, and their great legal powers have been given to them for that purpose. These two are in sympathy with the republican aristocratic group that is bitterly criticizing Caesar, and that is even now plotting his murder. They make references to the way in which these same craftsmen cheered Pompey's triumphal processions when he was the hero and darling of the Roman people not so long before. Though the craftsmen are quite flippant, they obey the tribunes and leave.

Flavius and Marullus then make it their business to remove the decorations (usually crowning wreaths or neck-garlands) from Caesar's statues and those of his relatives and ancestors.

Commentary

The opening scene in a Shakespearean play usually serves two functions. In the first place, it must make an immediate and powerful appeal to the audience's attention. This was especially important in the Elizabethan theater because of the informal, and sometimes rowdy, behavior of the play-goers. Here, Shakespeare gets their attention (and ours) at once with Flavius' opening, angry shouts at the "commoners." Secondly, Shakespeare's first scenes often give us some suggestion of the kind of situation, or theme, which is going to develop as the play goes on. For example, in Hamlet one of the main elements of the play is the dramatization of the hero's doubt and confusions, and the play opens with the tense, dramatic challenge and counter-challenge of some uneasy soldiers standing guard, suggesting to us at once that sense of confusion and uncertainty which will spread and intensify as the play continues. So here we have the two tribunes — Flavius and Marullus — who are not important as characters (they are "put to silence" in the next scene) but are dramatically significant because of what they say, against both Caesar and his plebeian admirers, and because they introduce us to the atmosphere of strife and disunity in Rome. It is an atmosphere that is only vague and general as yet, but that will become specific as the conspiracy of Cassius comes to light in the next scene.

The tribunes are the official representatives of the people, and are shown here as being violently opposed to Caesar because of his attempts to obtain absolute power in Rome by becoming a king. The Roman tradition was republican — government by the people, rather than a single authority — and it is this tradition that the tribunes here (and the Cassius-Brutus conspiracy later) are trying to uphold against the "royal" ambitions of Caesar.

All drama depends on conflict of some kind, both throughout the play as a whole, and in individual scenes. The conflict here is a verbal one between the tribunes and the cobbler. The tribunes have authority, and their language shows it ("You blocks, you stones, you worse than senseless things!") but against this authoritarian rhetoric Shakespeare puts the verbal cleverness of the cobbler, who exasperates Flavius and Marullus by his deliberate misunderstanding of what they say, and his habit of punning, and play on the meanings of the words he uses. When reading a Shakespeare play we must always remember that the language was meant to be heard and not read, and that puns spoken from the stage are more effective than they are on the printed page. As soon as the cobbler mentions "soles" he associates the word with "souls;" the phrase, "with the awl" suggests "withal." In playing on the various meanings he is able to 1) get the better of his social superiors, at least for some fifteen lines, and 2) thereby give a good deal of amusement to the large number of "commoners" like himself in the Elizabethan audience, who presumably had no more love for authority than does the cobbler.

In this scene Shakespeare makes another subtle but important point which prepares us for a crisis later in the play. The people have gathered "to see Caesar and rejoice in his triumph" in the traditional procession through the streets in honor of a returning hero. But Marullus points out how fickle their admiration is, for they had once welcomed Pompey with "an universal shout," just as they now welcome the man "who comes in triumph over Pompey's blood." On the stage before us the holiday mood of the crowd changes at once. Flavius notes, "They vanish tongue-tied in their guiltiness." Shakespeare impresses on us the way in which the crowd can be swayed since he wants us to recall this later in the play, at the climax of Act III, Scene 3, when Antony's speech converts the same crowd from the conspirators' cause to his own.

ACT I · SCENE 2

Summary

Caesar, accompanied by a crowd of friends and officials, proceeds to the Forum to celebrate the festival of Lupercal, during which, the younger public officials, stripped to the waist, participate in a foot race. Caesar calls upon his wife, Calphurnia, to stand within reach of the runners, and orders Antony, who is a consul and therefore one of the runners, not to forget to touch Calphurnia with his goatskin whip, since, according to folklore, the touch of a runner during this "holy chase" will cure a woman of barrenness.

The procession is about to move on when a soothsayer calls to Caesar to beware the Ides of March (March 15th). Caesar dismisses him contemptuously as a dreamer, and the procession continues.

Brutus and Cassius drop out of the company and admit to each other that they are not willing to be present if a crown is offered to Caesar, as it is rumored it will be. Cassius tries to learn Brutus' attitude toward Caesar, and when he finds that it is safe, reveals to him his own burning resentment at Caesar's dominance. He draws Brutus on to confess that, although he is fond of Caesar personally, he does not approve of Caesar's assumption of royal power. Cassius then reveals his own jealousy of Caesar, his contempt for Caesar's physical weaknesses, and his admiration of Brutus' qualities, which are suitable for leadership against tyranny. He compares Caesar with both himself and Brutus, and finds him no more remarkable than they are. It is their own lack of spirit which has allowed Caesar to grow so dominating, he contends. Though Brutus will not openly agree with all that Cassius urges, he listens and gives Cassius the impression that he is more than half persuaded to take Cassius' views and join him in acting against Caesar.

While they are conversing they twice hear loud shouts from the direction of the Forum, and each time Cassius becomes more definite and outspoken against Caesar, and Brutus more ready to listen.

The games over, the procession returns, with Caesar wearing an angry expression, Calphurnia pale, and Cicero apparently inwardly raging. Caesar notes Cassius' presence and, obviously suspicious of him, tells Antony that he distrusts thin, discontented-looking men like Cassius, but feels safe with sleek, fat men. Caesar does not fear Cassius but considers him dangerous. Antony assures him that Cassius is not dangerous, and the procession moves on.

Casca, at a hint from Brutus, remains behind and tells Brutus and Cassius what has taken place. Mark Antony three times offered Caesar a crownlike coronet. Each time Caesar put it aside, but each time more reluctantly, and each time the surrounding crowd shouted their approval more enthusiastically. Then Caesar fell to the ground and "foamed at the mouth and was speechless." Casca is contemptuous of the sweaty, evil-smelling mob, but when Cassius attempts to determine his political sympathies, he is too cautious to commit himself. He relates that Cicero, though, could not resist commenting on the play before his eyes, and for his own security spoke in Greek to his friends who understood and smiled, but did not speak. Brutus leaves after promising to consider what Cassius has said and to listen to him again the next day. Cassius, left alone, in a soliloquy shows that he is satisfied that he has influenced Brutus and will be able to win him over. He decides to forge, in various styles of handwriting, messages to the effect that Brutus is expected by many eminent citizens to take a stand against Caesar's so-called tyranny; then Cassius will throw these messages in Brutus' windows and leave them where he will find them.

Commentary

We ought to recall, at this point between Scenes 1 and 2, and indeed at every change of scene, that Shakespeare wrote for a theater which had nothing like our prolonged scene-changes, involving the lowering of a curtain and the changing of stage props and furnishings. On the Elizabethan stage, one scene ran directly into another, giving an effect rather like that of a moving picture dissolving from one shot to the next. The importance of this lies in the fact that Shakespeare often used the ending of one scene as a comment on, or introduction to, the next. Here, for example, Flavius and Marullus leave the stage at one side, talking of the man who would "keep us all in servile fearfulness" and immediately the object of their fear, Caesar himself, enters at the other side. Scene 1 had also prepared us for Scene 2 by giving us a general impression of fear and discord. Now that impression will gain sharper focus through the delineation of the principal characters — particularly Caesar, Cassius and Brutus.

This is Caesar's first appearance on the stage, but we must remember that the Elizabethan audience was familiar with his story, and that Shakespeare takes this familiarity into account and uses it. The Elizabethans were fascinated by Roman history, perhaps because they were themselves at this point creating an empire, and saw Rome both as a precedent and an analogy. For them, Caesar was, by definition, a monumental figure, "the foremost man of all this world" as Brutus calls him later in the play (Act IV, Sc. 3, 22). Therefore, Shakespeare did not have the task (as a modern playwright might have) of establishing Caesar's greatness. Assuming that his audience takes Caesar's stature for granted, he can go on to qualify and redefine the character for his own purposes in the play. Furthermore, to enlarge on the legendary Caesar — the hero and savior of Rome, pure and simple — would necessarily make the conspiracy against him a matter of irresponsible jealousy and viciousness. The conspirators must have some reason on their side, and we already know from Scene 1 that Caesar threatens both the liberty of the Roman citizens and the laws of the republic with his dictatorial designs. Now we are shown a Caesar in whom Shakespeare reveals, in one or two subtle details, the weakness that may accompany the will to dominate.

At one word from Caesar, the crowd is silenced by Casca, and Calphurnia and Antony are ordered to step forward. Caesar's authority is clear; it is asserted at once, and underlined by Antony's "When Caesar says 'Do this,' it is performed." We may recall at this point another Shakespearean ruler, who was also murdered. But in *Macbeth*, Duncan, the king, is deliberately made an example of both justice and gentleness in order to emphasize the enormity of Macbeth's crime. Caesar, on the other hand, is consciously arrogant; one feels, in what he says, his sense of being set apart from and above other men. Later on in this scene (11, 211 —‹12) he announces that, as Caesar, he is not "liable to fear" as others are: "I rather tell thee what is to be feared/Than what I fear; for always I am Caesar." Here, he disregards the soothsayer ("He is a dreamer") who warns him of the Ides of March. It is worth noting here that prophesies of this kind occur in several of Shakespeare's plays, always with the same dramatic function: dreams, omens, auguries, and indeed any sort of supernatural prediction are powerful devices for setting up a sense of dramatic anticipation in the audience — usually of some ominous or catastrophic event. Caesar's pride in disregarding any sort of warning or advice (here and in Act II, Sc. 2) is itself, we realize, an element in his downfall.

It is also significant that the soothsayer's warning is actually given to Caesar by Brutus. This is one example of the various kinds of dramatic irony that Shakespeare uses continually in his plays. Sometimes the irony is conscious (as when Cassius refers to "immortal Caesar" at the time when he is in fact planning Caesar's "mortality" or death), or the irony may be unconscious (understood in an ordinary sense by the characters on the stage, but in a further, ironic sense by us). Here, the friend who warns Caesar will become his assassin, as everyone in the audience knows. This is a minor example of dramatic irony, but Shakespeare was attentive to such details. There are more examples of this kind of irony later in the play.

Most of the scene is devoted to the dialogue between Cassius and Brutus, and these two major characters are carefully introduced and developed. Brutus' very first line is, as we have seen, an ironic touch. It is also a line that (as the critic-director, Sir Harley Granville-Barker, has pointed out) gives us something of the quality of Brutus himself: it is "measured, dispassionate, tinged with disdain." This quality — aloof, thoughtful, and perhaps a little cold — is expanded in Brutus' next lines. He is not "gamesome," nor does he have the "quick spirit" of Antony, and his first act is to attempt to leave the stage, but he is detained by Cassius.

The debate between Cassius and Brutus begins with Brutus' admission that he is "with himself at war," thereby giving Cassius his opportunity. From this point to line 161 Cassius does almost all the talking, and these hundred-odd lines are a masterful piece of insinuation and persuasion. Cassius goes to work cautiously, beginning with praise of Brutus' "hidden worthiness," and the respect the rest of Rome has for him. At one point, Cassius pauses ironically on Caesar's "immortal," or godlike, quality; but he is too careful to enlarge on the subject until Brutus himself brings it up, and this happens at line 81, with the offstage shouts from the crowd.These two shouts are carefully placed in the development of the argument. They both bring forth almost involuntary responses from Brutus that show us that he, too, has Caesar and his ambition in mind. To Brutus' first reaction — "I do fear the people/Choose Caesar for their king'' — Cassius replies with great care: "Then must I think you would not have it so.'' It is important for his purpose to make Brutus, rather than himself, the one who first suggests the danger of Caesar. He succeeds in this, but is too clever to press the point home. Instead, he takes up a phrase used by Brutus — "the name of honor'' — and moves toward his subject from another direction. Brutus has said that the notion of honor is close to his heart, and Cassius next associates honor with the idea of freedom, and specifically with freedom from Caesar (Act I, Sc. 2, 97-99). The story of Cassius' rescue of Caesar from the Tiber follows, and in it two points are made. The first (and most obvious) is the reduction of Caesar from godlike superiority to human frailty (one imagines Cassius' disdain when he remarks: "'Tis true, this god did shake!''); the second point lies in Cassius' reminder to Brutus, through the figure of Aeneas, "our great ancestor,'' of the founding of Rome, and the whole Roman heritage. For Brutus this means the tradition of republican freedom, and Cassius reminds him later of the fact that his own ancestors had defended this freedom against the royalist Tarquins. Throughout his account of the Tiber incident, Cassius increases the force and bitterness of his attack until, at Brutus' reaction to the offstage shout, his voice rises to the fury of "Why, man, he doth bestride the narrow world/Like a Colossus. . . .''

Notice that once Cassius has attacked Caesar directly, the whole tone of his argument changes. At the outset, he spoke vaguely of his own "worthy cogitations'' and asserted that "honor is the subject of my story.'' His appeal was to Brutus' general sense of right and wrong. But once he is assured that Brutus will listen to him, his appeals to justice and morality are increasingly accompanied by personal hatred and envy. The great Caesar is "of feeble temper,'' "a sick girl,'' while he and Brutus "peep about/To find ourselves dishonorable graves.'' We already know the ambition of Caesar, the man in power. In some of Cassius' speeches we begin to see the ambition of the man excluded from power, and his frustration: "The fault, dear Brutus, is not in our stars/But in ourselves, that we are underlings.''

Brutus' attitude throughout all this has been non-commital. He is at first puzzled by Cassius ("What is it that you would impart to me?''), and it is part of the purpose of the scene to indicate Brutus' simplicity in matters of political intrigue. The very manner in which Cassius develops his argument is that of a practiced manipulator working on an innocent subject. We are by no means certain just how far Brutus has understood Cassius, and it is part of Shakespeare's design to keep us uncertain: Brutus would not be Brutus if he realized Cassius' plan at once and fell in with it. The speech in answer to Cassius beginning at line 162 does not seem to tell us much: Brutus shares "some aim'' with Cassius, but does not wish to be "any further moved.'' The content of the speech is vague and ambiguous, but Shakespeare often tells us much about a character through the form, or manner in which he speaks. Here the phrases and sentences are brief, the rhythms short and choppy, all suggesting tight, controlled, difficult speech. Compare the confident, impassioned rhythms of Cassius, and his long, powerful phrases. Brutus' language and delivery are those of a man laboring in the uncertainty of a powerful conflict. He ends with the uneasy and inconclusive assertion that "no son of Rome" should accept the "hard conditions" of the time.

Caesar's party returns to the stage, and Caesar's remarks concerning Cassius confirm much of what we had inferred from the earlier dialogue. The "lean and hungry look" is a subtle direction from Shakespeare as to how the actor should play the role. The cleverness that Caesar notes in Cassius where human actions and motives are concerned ("he looks/Quite through the deeds of men") is clear to us after hearing his analysis of Caesar himself, and watching his artful handling of Brutus. Finally it is, of course, ironic that it is Caesar himself who sees the threat of Cassius most clearly: "Such men are dangerous." Yet Caesar's own pride, given aggressive expression in his next speech (Act I, Sc. 2, 198-214) makes it impossible for him to see the danger he is in.

Casca is drawn aside by Brutus and Cassius to report to them (and to us) what has been happening offstage. Casca speaks in prose for two reasons: i) he is described as "sour" and "blunt," and represents a fairly common type on the Elizabethan stage — the cynical realist with harsh speech and irritating manner — who is suited better to prose than to more polished and formal blank verse, and ii) the rhythms of iambic pentameter, or blank verse, despite Shakespeare's flexible and varied handling of it, can develop a certain monotony over long periods on the stage, and we have just had more than two hundred lines of it. The prose of the next sixty lines gives us a rhythmic change of pace.

In making Casca a rough-tongued cynic, Shakespeare departs from his source in Plutarch, and he does so in order to give us, through Casca, a pessimistic and disillusioned view of Caesar. In Casca's report, Caesar is a demagogue. Offered a crown, Caesar "would fain have had it" until he sensed the people's displeasure, at which point he made the dramatic gesture described in lines 260-61, apparently with such a show of sincerity that, had Casca been an ordinary member of the crowd, "I would I might go to hell" rather than have disbelieved him. Casca's reference to the "tag-rag people" clapping as though they were in a theater is a significant underlining of an impression we get throughout: Caesar regarding himself as a heroic actor, and playing to an audience. Casca is equally hard on the people themselves. If Caesar is a fake, then they are dupes, and his contempt is summed up in the lines describing the girls who hear Caesar's apology and cry:

> 'Alas, good soul!,' and forgave him with all their hearts. But there's no need to be taken of them. If Caesar had stabbed their mothers, they would have done no less.

It is an unflattering portrait of a mob, but necessary to Shakespeare's purposes later in Act III, Sc. 2 and 3, where both the mob's fickleness and its brutality play an important part. At the end of his account, Casca adds, off-handedly, a last detail, and it is the more powerful for being off-handed. Marullus and Flavius, Casca says, "for pulling scarfs off Caesar's images, are put to silence." Having seen Caesar the demagogue, we are reminded again of the efficient brutality with which his regime operates.

Shakespeare builds his characters and develops his themes in careful, subtle touches, and we notice one here, after Casca leaves. Brutus remarks on the way Casca has changed since his youth. Where he was once "quick" he is now "blunt." But Cassius at once points out that this is only a "form" or pretence — which Cassius sees through — and we recall Caesar's remark about Cassius' ability to "look quite through the deeds of men." In contrast to Brutus (and they are contrasted throughout the first half of the play), Cassius is the astute judge of men and situations. It will be he who sees the threat of Antony, and the danger of letting him live to speak at Caesar's funeral. It is Cassius who is the practical mind of the conspiracy, and Brutus who, though he brings to it all his integrity, perhaps does not fully understand its working.

Brutus leaves, and Cassius speaks the soliloquy which closes the scene, and is the first soliloquy of the play. The soliloquy — in which the actor, alone on the stage, speaks his thoughts directly to the audience — was one of the most useful devices of the Elizabethan theater, and one which modern realistic playwrights badly miss. The soliloquy could do several things. It might give us a new insight to the character who speaks it, or provide a general comment on the progress of the action. Cassius' soliloquy does both. Certainly he reveals a good deal about himself: here he is a vindictive and cold-blooded schemer. In part, his villainy here stimulates the dramatic movement of the play; the audience wants to see just how it will be put into action. The Cassius of the scenes to come is never quite as Machiavellian as this again. The soliloquy also serves to prepare us directly for the organization of the conspiracy, and it ends with a ringing prediction of the troubles to come. When we recall the almost instantaneous scene-changes in the Elizabethan theater, we realize that the "thunder" which introduces scene three will begin to roll, with ominous effect, on Cassius' final words, " . . . or worse days endure."

ACT I · SCENE 3

Summary

A fearful storm is raging as the scene opens. Cicero, a senator, meets Casca, who is terror-struck and has his sword drawn. Casca relates to Cicero the supernatural phenomena which have occurred: the rain of fire, the quaking of the earth, the hand of a common slave which flamed "like twenty torches joined" and yet remained unscorched, the lion near the Capitol which gazed at Casca and passed by him, the walking dead, and the owl that hooted at noon in the market place. Casca believes all these events to be ill omens.

Cicero is unmoved and ambiguously agrees that times are strange indeed. Then he asks Casca whether Caesar will be at the Capitol the next day to meet the Senate. Casca informs him that he will, and Cicero leaves him to find shelter.

Cassius enters, recognizes Casca by voice, and finding Casca so terrified, attempts to enlist him into his conspiracy. First he describes how he himself has gone through a storm with bare breast inviting the lightning to strike him. To Casca's incredulous question as to why he has done so rash a thing to tempt the gods, Cassius answers that Casca ought to know that it is the anger of the gods over the state of affairs in Rome that is shown in this disturbance in the heavens, and that he can name the man responsible. Casca, off his guard, blurts out "Caesar."

Cassius throws away caution and makes a genuinely passionate speech, declaring he will kill himself rather than live in Rome under a tyranny. Casca agrees and enthusiastically pledges his support to the conspiracy.

Cinna, another conspirator, enters and comments that it is a "fearful night." Cassius sends Cinna to distribute his forged letters where Brutus will find them. Afterward, they will meet at Pompey's Porch. When Cinna leaves, Cassius takes Casca with him to Brutus' house. Casca approves of Brutus as the leader because of the latter's great reputation for uprightness, which will give the color of patriotism to all they do. Cassius states his intention of finishing the job of winning over Brutus to their cause.

Commentary

Scene 3 gives us one of the many examples of the way in which Shakespeare compresses historical or chronological time as he sees fit, in order to give us a sense of dramatic continuity. Historically, the Feast of Lupercal and the eve of the Ides of March (respectively Scenes 2 and 3 of this Act) were separated by about a month. But Shakespeare's dramatic imagination runs them together so that the "worse days" that Cassius predicts are with us immediately in the "thunder and lightning" of the opening of Scene 3.

Readers of Shakespeare may wonder why, since he wrote for an open theater in which performances were given in the afternoon, he wrote so many night scenes. But neither Shakespeare nor his audience worried about the sort of realistic imitation of night that the theatrical electricians can produce on our stage. Shakespeare creates night, as he creates so many other things on his stage, through language; and he can create, as the electricians cannot, many different kinds, or variations, of night and darkness. It may be the romantic night which surrounds the lovers in the Act V of *The Merchant of Venice*, where

The moon shines bright: in such a night as this
When the sweet wind did gently kiss the trees . . .

Or it may be evil, as is the night in which Lady MacBeth contemplates the murder of Duncan:

> Come thick night,
> And pall me in the dunnest smoke of hell,
> That my keen knife sees not the wound it makes . . .

Or it may be ominous and terrifying, as in this scene,

> this dreadful night
> That thunders, lightens, opens graves, and roars
> As doth the lion in the Capitol . . .

Night provides an important atmospheric, or symbolic, setting in Shakespeare: it is often associated with evil. Here, as in *Macbeth*, night provides an appropriate background for the lurking, plotting conspirators. It also suggests, as Brutus says in Act II, Sc. 1, a time "when evil is most free." The storm is also important, and the stage directions remind us that it continues through this scene, through the next scene with Brutus, and to the scene after that with Caesar, thus linking the three together. Storm in Shakespeare's plays carried a significance that is largely lost for us. The Elizabethans thought of individual man, his society (or "the state"), and the natural world as intimately and indivisibly connected. Therefore disorder and violence in the world of nature suggested, and on the stage could represent, disorder in the society and the individual. For the Elizabethans the king symbolized the state, and therefore when the king is murdered (i.e., when the social order is violently disrupted) in *Macbeth*, we have a storm ("the heavens, as troubled by man's act/Threaten his bloody stage") much like the storm here, with its "monstrous prodigies." In both cases violence, murder, and consequent social disorder are at hand. In the same way, the individual was often compared to nature and to society: disorder in one might be used to express disorder in the other. Thus when Brutus agonizes over his part in the plot against Caesar he compares himself to a society in conflict:

> the state of man,
> Like to a little kingdom, suffers then
> The nature of an insurrection. (Act II, Sc. 1, 67-69)

Since the actual violence of the storm cannot be reproduced on the Elizabethan stage, Shakespeare, as usual, communicates it through the effect it has on a character. Casca, running onto the stage with a drawn sword, says that "all the sway of earth/Shakes like a thing unfirm," and goes on to give a vivid description of the tempest that we cannot see but can, with him, imagine. Note that Casca here speaks in blank verse rather than the prose we had associated with him in Act I, Sc. 2. The reason for this is two-fold.

Firstly, the kind of terrifying and supernatural occurrences treated here need the special elevation and rhythmic movement of poetry. Secondly, it is significant that it should be Casca, earlier represented as tough and unimpressionable, who is so shaken by these omens; it gives them added force for us.

The imagery throughout this passage (Act I, Sc. 3, 3-13, 15-32) has an intense and nightmarish quality. The "tempest dropping fire" is no ordinary lightning storm, and is followed by the figure of a man holding up his hand "which did flame and burn/Like twenty torches joined." This image, and that of the lion which follows it, are both associated in our minds with destruction and violence, and these are in turn followed by a powerful suggestion of general terror and desolation in the "hundred ghastly women,/Transformed with their fear" whom Casca next sees. The passage ends with a reference to the owl, "the bird of night," a traditional omen of evil for the Elizabethan audience.

Professor Wilson Knight has shown the way in which the ideas and images of music and storm recur in Shakespeare's plays in such a way that the first is associated with goodness and harmony, the second with evil and strife. We were told in Scene 2 that Cassius "hears no music" and we are not surprised now when he welcomes the storm (Act I, Sc. 3, 45-52). It reflects his own mood of overpowering, destructive anger. He sees it, as he sees everything at this point in the play, in relation to Caesar, and he takes advantage of Casca's fear to enlist him among the conspirators. Notice that once this has been done, both behave with an obviously tense, conspiratorial quality. They are afraid to be seen ("Stand close") when Cinna enters, and once they recognize him and all draw together the dialogue is conducted with nervous urgency. Cinna wants to be certain who Casca is; Cassius has to repeat his question to Cinna; and finally Cassius gives his orders concerning the letters to Brutus in brief, hurried phrases. The conspirators have completed their plans to make Brutus a central figure in their plot, but as they congratulate themselves on this, the audience senses a typical touch of dramatic irony when it is realized how misplaced the conspirators' optimism is.

ACT II · SCENE 1

Summary

Brutus is sleepless, still making up his mind about the conspiracy after his evening's interview with Cassius. He calls his slave-boy Lucius to light a candle in his study, and when Lucius does so he finds one of Cassius' anonymous letters to Brutus. Brutus has found several of them before. While Lucius is out, Brutus reviews his reasons for joining this conspiracy to murder Caesar. These are that, though for himself he has no cause to murder Caesar, yet for the good of the state it must be done, because the absolute power of a king may change his nature and make him oppressive and tyrannical. Therefore, he must be prevented from having this chance and this

35

temptation. The fallacy in his reasoning is that Caesar is to be killed not for what he has done but for what he may do; also, Caesar as king could hardly have any more absolute power than he has at the moment.

Cassius and five other conspirators (Casca, Decius, Cinna, Metellus and Trebonius) arrive and are admitted. Each of them is presented by Cassius to Brutus, though he is acquainted with them all. In a whispered conversation Cassius brings Brutus up to date on the progress of events while the others discuss the time of sunrise — a trivial point.

Brutus and Cassius having finished their conversation, Brutus clasps the hands of all of them once more, but refuses to hear of an oath being sworn among such a band of high-souled brothers. He has already assumed the lead with the implied consent of Cassius, who feels they need Brutus at all costs. Brutus makes his first mistake in this matter of the oath, because one of this group will betray their confidence before daylight to Artemidorus, a teacher of rhetoric, who, having the details of the plot, will try to get Caesar to read a note containing them. It is only fate and Caesar's careless self-assurance which will prevent the whole plot from being exposed then and there.

Cassius then proposes that Cicero be included in the conspiracy, and is seconded by the others. Brutus makes his second mistake and vetoes the suggestion on the grounds that Cicero will have nothing to do with an enterprise he has not initiated himself. The others quickly change their tune and fall in line, showing just how highly they regard Brutus. So the master-orator of the age is excluded, and they find out later that they have no one to offset the influence of Mark Antony's eloquence upon the populace, and that is the beginning of their downfall.

Cassius then suggests that Mark Antony should be killed at the same time as Caesar, because, devoted as he is to Caesar, he may prove a shrewd and dangerous enemy to them later. Brutus vetoes this suggestion too, on the grounds that when Caesar is gone Antony will be helpless and no menace, and anyway, he is a useless trifler, incapable of making himself a threat. Later, it is the same Antony who checkmates them and starts them on the slippery path to their doom.

Cassius is not sure that Caesar will attend the Senate meeting. Decius volunteers to have him there. He will call and bring him. Cassius decides that they will all be there, and Brutus names the time: the eighth hour.

Metellus suggests that Caius Ligarius be included in their number. Brutus promises to persuade him and Metellus is requested to send for him at once. At three o'clock the conspirators break up to meet at Caesar's house.

Portia, Brutus' wife (also his first cousin) enters and begins to complain to him that she is being excluded from his confidence: He has not been himself recently, preoccupied, moody, silent to her and sleepless. She claims the right as his loyal wife to know what is in his mind and heart. Is she not Cato's daughter, one of the giants of Roman public life universally revered, and is she not his wife? She shows a gash she has purposely given herself in her thigh just to prove that she can stand pain and exercise self-control as well as a man. Brutus is deeply touched and promises to share all his secrets with her.

Just at this moment Ligarius is shown in with his head bandaged. He has been ill, but rises from his sick-bed at the word of Brutus. The latter mentions an enterprise of vast importance. Ligarius suspects what it is, and throws away his head bandages. As they go out, Brutus is starting to explain the conspiracy to Ligarius.

Commentary

The stormy night continues, and Brutus' first lines refer to the surrounding darkness. Darkness throughout this scene is given a subtle but important symbolic significance. It represents, or suggests to the imagination, the darkness and the confusion in Brutus' mind. Later on the conspirators arrive in darkness, and one feels that night (and its association with secrecy and evil) gives a sinister quality to everything they say and do. Compare the same effect when Macbeth plots the murder of Duncan:

Now o'er one half the world
Nature seems dead, and wicked dreams abuse
The curtained sleep.

Brutus calls to Lucius, his servant boy, for light. Here too some critics have seen symbolic significance. Brutus, in a darkness both actual and mental, asks the boy for illumination. Lucius' name is derived from the Latin word for light (*Lucere*: to light), and in a sense he represents the illumination, or understanding, that Brutus needs. Yet Brutus never reaches the "light" provided by Lucius in the study; instead he is interrupted by the conspirators, coming "by night,/When evils are most free." Throughout the play Lucius, although a minor character, is important in that he shows us the serenity and peace of mind that Brutus has lost. Sleep in Shakespeare is often associated with peace, and Lucius can sleep when Brutus cannot (both here, and in Act IV, Sc. 3). Brutus, awake and harassed by anxiety, half-recognizes the contrast between Lucius' innocent sleep and his own guilty wakefulness when he compares "the honey-heavy dew of slumber" with the "fantasies" and "busy care" that plague him (Act II, Sc. 1, 230-2). Brutus' dealings with the boy (and with Portia) reflect his gentleness and humanity. Some directors of the play have given Lucius the part of Strato, so that, at the end of the play, it is Lucius who holds the sword on which Brutus kills himself (thus, he finally provides that "sleep" of peace which is the only thing that Brutus, broken and defeated, really desires).

Brutus' soliloquy (beginning at line 10) is an important one. It is an example of Shakespeare's brilliance in revealing ambiguous or confused states of mind, where the confusion or ambiguity is not clearly realized by the speaker himself. The heroes of Shakespeare's tragedies are often in the position of making decisions which will ultimately destroy them, and the real nature of which they do not themselves understand. By the language they use, Shakespeare manages to suggest both their surface certainty, and their unconscious doubt or confusion. In this speech Brutus seems certain of what he has to do. He begins, in fact, with a final decision: "It must be by his death." But when he proceeds to his reasons, or justifications, Shakespeare makes them doubtful, although understandable. Brutus, the man of honor, says he has no "personal cause" for destroying Caesar (and we compare him with Cassius, whose personal hatred was made clear in Act I, Sc. 2). Brutus goes on to say that Caesar must die because he will abuse his power. Yet he adds at once that he has no evidence that Caesar ever behaved unreasonably. The two remarks about "bright day" bringing forth "the adder," and "young ambition's ladder" both have the quality of conventional phrases: they are plausible excuses, not logical arguments. Then Brutus significantly admits that the "quarrel" really has no "color" — or excuse — as it stands. He is compelled to "fashion it," or put it in some other, more acceptable way. And he ends up unconsciously admitting that in order to be able to act he must, in a sense, distort his view of Caesar: "therefore think him as a serpent's egg." As Brutus argues with (and convinces) himself of his course of action, we realize the basic uncertainty of his position.

Lines 55-8 of Act II, Sc. 1 are understood ironically by the audience, though not by Brutus. "Redress" means revenge, and "thy full petition" means that Rome will get from Brutus all it asks for. This is true in a sense other than Brutus intends; what Rome will ultimately ask for is Brutus' life.

As Lucius leaves to bring in Cassius and the other conspirators, Brutus' speech (Act II, Sc. 1, 76-85) indicates the way in which he, the model of moral correctness, has compromised himself. Throughout the play he insists (and we believe him) on his integrity and honesty, and, as he says here, conspiracy is ashamed to show its "monstrous visage" and must "hide in smiles and affability." We remember this as Brutus advances to greet the conspirators and make himself one of them. He is himself now among the "secret Romans," and we wonder how this new role will fit in with his morality.

While Brutus and Cassius withdraw at one point, presumably while Cassius makes sure of Brutus' support, Decius, Casca and Cinna talk, apparently quite irrelevantly, about which direction the sun will rise. As with many apparent irrelevancies in Shakespeare, this one has dramatic value. Men under extreme stress frequently ease themselves with this kind of aimless talk, and the references to the rising of the sun ("Doth not the day break here?"), like the reference to the Ides of March, earlier, sharpens the dramatic anticipation of the audience: the day of the assassination is beginning.

The conspirators now discuss their next moves, and here we watch Brutus make two judgments which 1) tell us something about the man, and 2) by implication, suggest that the plot against Caesar is on unsure ground because of Brutus' judgment. We have already seen, in Cassius' and Brutus' analysis of Casca (Act I, Sc. 2), some of the differences between the two men: Cassius, with practical intelligence "looking quite through the deeds of men," Brutus, high-minded and utterly sincere, yet without the shrewdness to judge men's behavior, or the tactical requirements of political action. Cassius suggests that Cicero ought to be included, and Metellus seconds this, because the "good opinion" Rome has of Cicero "will commend our deeds." We have seen Cicero earlier, during the storm, where his calmness was in noticeable contrast to Casca's fear and excitement. Furthermore, the name of Cicero stands, for the Elizabethans and for us, for intelligent Roman statesmanship. We feel that Metellus is right, but Brutus at once rejects his suggestion with the brisk "name him not!," followed by a reason that is doubtful at best. Next, Cassius brings up the question of Mark Antony, observing with sour wit that since Antony and Caesar are so close, it seems a shame to let one outlive the other. Faced with the decision, Brutus makes what will prove to be a fatal mistake. Since Antony is given "To sports, to wildness, and much company" he can be dismissed as a threat. Brutus, by nature, is somewhat righteous and oversimplifies characters unlike his own. In shrugging Antony off as a harmless pleasure-seeker, he makes a judgment that will return, quite literally, to haunt him (Act IV, Sc. 3). Cassius, on the other hand, rightly estimates the danger in Antony's "ingrafted love" for Caesar.

One other point occurs in this debate which further enlarges our understanding of Brutus. We know that he believes his part in the conspiracy to be morally justifiable; but we have also seen, in his soliloquy, something like uncertainty, or guilt, which he has tried to dismiss. He must at all costs make the assassination an act of public morality. In his speech (Act II, Sc. 1, 162-83) he introduces the idea of religious sacrifice. The conspirators will be "sacrificers, but not butchers" and "carve" Caesar in a way which is "fit for the gods,/Not hew him as a carcass fit for hounds." Brutus cannot stomach the deed if it is not performed as an almost religious duty. Again he seems to be trying to avoid, or not face directly, the violence and bloody nature of the deed. But we shall see later that the hunt is exactly the metaphor that Antony uses in describing the dead Caesar, the "brave hart" surrounded by the "hunters" and "bloody butchers."

The conspirators leave, and Brutus is left alone with Lucius. Brutus turns to make a command to the boy but, finding him asleep, he stops and compares the boy's peace to his own turmoil as Portia enters. Between them, Portia and Lucius suggest to us all that is, or might have been, normal and happy in Brutus' life. They stand as a contrast to the world of the conspiracy, the struggles of conscience, and the violence of assassination and battle. Lucius we have already discussed, but Portia requires some comment.

The play is predominantly about men, and their struggle for power; therefore a large part of it is concerned with debate, planning and battle. Brutus appears most of the time as a public figure, surrounded by men and concerned in affairs of state. But in order to give depth and humanity to his character Shakespeare introduces Portia so that we may see Brutus in a very different context: a man who has a home and a wife whom he loves, and who loves him.

Women's parts were, of course, taken by boys on the Elizabethan stage, and this presented a problem to the dramatist. He was obliged to keep his female characters relatively simple, since a boy-actor could not be expected to do justice to the complex moods and emotions of a Prince Hamlet or a King Lear. It is true that Shakespeare has, on at least two occasions, given us women of great power; but even Lady Macbeth and Cleopatra, although impressive, are far simpler, as characters, than most of the male creations. Making, as usual, a virtue out of necessity, Shakespeare converts the youth and limitations of his boy-actors into heroines who are simple, straightforward, and innocent: Cordelia, Desdemona, Miranda, and here, Portia.

In this scene Portia also reminds us, by her love and concern for her troubled husband, that Brutus has been happy and contented in a period before the play began. This gives added pathos to the desperate and destructive course he now seems to have taken. When the death of Portia herself is announced later in the play, we realize more fully the dimensions of the destruction he has brought about. Brutus' tragedy is both a public one (in effect, he destroys the thing he is trying to preserve, for republican freedom falls to the domination of the triumvirate) and a private one (the death of Portia, and his happiness). It is the private aspect that is prepared for in this scene.

Portia reminds Brutus that she is Cato's daughter, and Cato the Elder has always served as a symbol of Roman strength and courage. Shakespeare incorporates into Portia's speech a detail taken from Plutarch, and meant to exemplify the sort of stern self-discipline associated with Cato. This is the "voluntary wound" which, according to Plutarch, Portia gave herself to convince Brutus of her loyalty.

> She took a razor, and causing her maids and women to go out of her chamber, she gave herself a great gash in her thigh, that she was straight covered with blood . . . and spake in this sort to Brutus: 'I being, Brutus, the daughter of Cato, was married to thee not to be thy bed-fellow and companion at board only, but to be partaker with thee of good and evil fortune . . . I have found that no pain and grief can overcome me.' With these words she showed him her wound, and told him what she had done to prove herself. Brutus besought the gods that he might be found a husband worthy of so noble a wife as Portia.
>
> (Plutarch: *Life of Brutus*)

Shakespeare takes the character of Portia straight from Plutarch's account; but notice the way he minimizes the details of the "voluntary wound," and enlarges on the humanity and tenderness of Brutus' wife.

What is the significance of the Ligarius episode which ends the scene? Is Ligarius' recovery from his illness some sort of miraculous testimony to the healing qualities of Brutus? Or are we meant to understand, on the other hand, that just because of his nobility Brutus' enthusiasm may be a little *too* catching? Certainly there is more emotion than reason in Ligarius' statement that, so long as it is Brutus who leads, he will follow "To do I know not what."

ACT II · SCENE 2

Summary

Having just been present at a domestic scene of particular charm and sweetness in Brutus' house, we are now spectators at one in Caesar's house. Caesar, in his dressing gown, has been awakened by the storm and Calphurnia crying out in her sleep that Caesar is being murdered. He orders a servant to tell the priests to present sacrifices and read the omens.

Calphurnia enters in great agitation and tells Caesar he must not leave the house this day. She has just been hearing from someone on watch about all the happenings that have appeared in the streets and the sky and, contrary to her habit, she is frightened for Caesar. Caesar dismisses her fears and states his intention of going out no matter what.

The servant brings word from the priests that the omens are unfavorable; they have sacrificed a beast that had no heart, and Caesar must not stir out of the house. Caesar dismisses these omens too, but Calphurnia, in desperation, kneels to him — just as Portia kneeled to Brutus — and begs that he do as she asks and send Mark Antony to say Caesar is not well. Caesar is touched and, lifting her up, he agrees to take her advice, respect her fears, and send Mark Antony to say he is not well.

Just then Decius is admitted. Caesar commissions him to tell the Senate he will not be present this day. To Calphurnia's urging that Decius say he is sick, Decius replies that he scorns to send a lie. Decius begs to have some reason to give the Senate. Caesar says that it is enough to tell the Senate that it is his will, but Caesar explains for Decius' private satisfaction that Calphurnia has had a terrible dream that Caesar's statue spouted a hundred streams of blood and many Romans joyfully bathed their hands in it. Decius attempts to interpret the dream, not as a warning of calamity, but as a good sign that Caesar shall revive the commonwealth. He adds the news that the Senate intends to grant him a crown at this session. Caesar runs the risk of being thought afraid, he says. Caesar changes his mind and makes light to Calphurnia of her dream and her fears. He decides to go to the Senate.

A senator named Publius is admitted at the same time as the rest of the conspirators. Caesar, the most polished gentleman in Rome, thanks them for their courtesy in thus coming to attend him and sets out for the Senate accompanied by them all.

Commentary

The opening stage direction calling for thunder and lightning joins this scene with the previous one. The storm beneath which Brutus and Caius Ligarius leave the stage continues as Caesar enters, and the symbolic association of the storm with violence in the world of men is present again at the beginning of this scene. The two scenes are linked in another way. We have just seen Brutus and Portia; now we have Caesar and his wife, Calphurnia. In both cases the women are fearful: Portia senses intuitively that something is wrong, and Calphurnia has had a frightening dream. In both cases the men disregard their wives, and proceed with their chosen courses of action toward their fatal meeting.

Calphurnia's recital of the "horrid sights seen by the watch" intensifies our anticipation of the events to come, and is another example of Shakespeare's use of the unnatural or supernatural to surround the murder of kings or rulers with a special aura of terror. He seems to have associated the idea of unnatural portents with Caesar's death in particular, and returns to it again in *Hamlet*, a play written immediately after *Julius Caesar*:

In the most high and palmy state of Rome,
A little ere the mightiest Julius fell,
The graves stood tenantless and the sheeted dead
Did squeak and gibber in the Roman streets;
As stars with trains of fire and dews of blood,
Disasters in the sun; and the moist star
Upon whose influence Neptune's empire stands
Was sick almost to doomsday with eclipse. (Act I, Sc. 1, 112-18)

Shakespeare dwells on these chaotic omens to remind us that Caesar's murder is not simply an individual act of violence. For the Elizabethan audience, the overthrow of the ruler or king also destroyed the peace and harmony of the state or society. The "fierce fiery warriors," the noise of battle and the groans of dying men are portents suggesting the civil strife and bloody conflict that necessarily (to the Elizabethan mind) followed the act of rebellion, or the murder of the head of state. Hence these omens and portents of Calphurnia's are important for the whole play as they impress upon us that — despite the integrity of Brutus — what is being planned is bound to produce war and bloodshed. We shall not be surprised at Antony's predictions in Act III, Sc. 1.

Shakespeare's presentation of Caesar in this scene is particularly skillful. He is able to suggest both the self-consciously public figure — the hero to whom fear is unknown — yet also the private individual who yields to his wife's fear (which is also, perhaps, his own). At first Caesar treats the omens as meaningless, and makes them the basis for a typical display of pride: he is "more dangerous" and "elder and more terrible" than danger itself. We are reminded of Cassius' suggestion earlier of Caesar's overwhelming egotism.

Yet as soon as Calphurnia says "Call it my fear," Caesar pacifies her, and here we have the suggestion of another side of Caesar that we have not seen: he is not only the Colossus that "bestrides the narrow world," but also a man, here moved by the obvious distress of his wife. However, with the entrance of Decius, Caesar reasserts the character of the monumental public hero. Unable to make an excuse that might suggest some human weakness, he relies on pride: he is too great to be obliged to explain himself. Calphurnia's interruption ("Say he is sick") is unfortunate in that it forces Caesar to expand on his superiority to the "greybeards" (senators). He is now in a perfect position to be weakened by implied threats to this superiority. It is this arrogance that gives Decius his opportunity; he has already told us that he can manipulate Caesar, and now we see this ability at work. There are two things which Caesar's sort of pride cannot stand. One is ridicule, and we note Decius' careful insertion of "Lest I be laughed at" at line 70 where the meaning is really you and not I. The other is contempt, and Decius, at the end of his speech, is able to suggest that Caesar i) is dependent upon his wife's dreams for his decisions, and ii) is, quite simply, afraid. Decius gives a masterly performance throughout, particularly in his rapidly improvised interpretation of Calphurnia's dream, of Caesar's statue "that did run pure blood." This piece of description is, of course, dramatically important since it anticipates for us the actual event in Act III, Sc. 1.

The conspirators enter, and Caesar orders wine to be prepared for them. This is a subtle touch on Shakespeare's part. We know that Caesar is ambitious, and we know that Brutus honestly believes that he must die for the general good. Yet we have seen Caesar earlier in this scene calming the fears of his wife, and we see him now as a man and a host, offering wine to his murderers. As one of the play's directors has pointed out, the wine has the effect of a "sacrament of trust;" whatever we think of Brutus' integrity, we cannot help but react to the sight of the killers drinking with their unsuspecting victim. Perhaps we recall that, besides Brutus' honesty, the conspiracy comes also from the envy of Cassius and the mixed motives of the rest (see Act V, Sc. 5, 69-72). The lines spoken in asides at the end of the scene may also make a distinction between Brutus and the rest of the conspiracy. Trebonius delivers his with something like a snarl of hatred, while Brutus' emotion is, typically, one of sorrow for what he has to do.

ACT II · SCENE 3

Summary

While Caesar is setting out from his house we are presented with a street scene near the Capitol. Artemidorus, a teacher of rhetoric, has found out the names of all eight conspirators and he lists them. Apparently he knows the part assigned to each one also, and this information could only have come from one of the eight. He posts himself in a spot from which he will be able to hand Caesar a note as he passes.

Commentary

The conspirators are prepared, and their plans are in motion; Decius has persuaded Caesar to go to the Senate. The last two scenes of Act II provide a kind of bridge between the time of Caesar's leaving his house, and his arrival at the Capitol. The characters that appear — Artemidorus in this scene, Portia and the soothsayer in the next — all have some knowledge or suspicion of the approaching crisis, and they communicate their apprehension to us.

Here Artemidorus has a special function. We have heard a great deal from the anti-Caesar faction in support of the assassination. From Artemidorus we are given an indication of what other Romans might say for and in defence of Caesar. We have no reason to doubt Artemidorus' honesty, and he sees the conflict as between Caesar's "virtue" and the "traitors" who threaten him. This sort of qualification to the view of Caesar as a complete tyrant prevents us from seeing the problem in oversimplifications of good and bad.

ACT II · SCENE 4

Summary

Portia shows in this scene that she has been told the details of the plot. Her agitation on account of her husband is so acute that she cannot sit still to await the outcome and sends Lucius off to the Capitol, though in her excitement she forgets to tell him what to do. Finally she orders him to observe how things are going with Brutus and what Caesar does, and at last to give Brutus her love and say she is merry and bring back his answer.

The soothsayer enters and is questioned by Portia for news. She wants to know whether he has been at the Capitol; then the time, then whether Caesar has gone to the Capitol or not. He answers that it is the ninth hour and that Caesar has not yet gone to the Capitol. She wants to know whether the soothsayer has a favor to ask of Caesar and when he says he has one which concerns his personal interest very nearly, she takes alarm at the thought that the secret may be out. When she realizes from his reply that he does not know of the plot but fears one, she almost faints from relief. Her next sentence shows that she knows the details, "Brutus hath a suit that Caesar will not grant." Finally, she feels herself fainting and goes into the house.

Commentary

This scene is based on a brief passage in Plutarch's *Life of Brutus*, and it is interesting to see what Shakespeare makes of it. The passage in Plutarch goes, in part:

> Portia was frighted with every noise and cry she heard . . . and sent messenger after messenger, to know what news. Her weakness was not able to hold out any longer, and thereupon she suddenly swooned.

Shakespeare's Portia has only one messenger, but she shows her anxiety in her urgent, unthinking demands to Lucius to "run to the Senate house." The short, breathless phrases in lines 13-16 suggest her agitation, verging on incoherence. From Plutarch's "frighted with every noise" Shakespeare imagines the dialogue in lines 16-19. Portia's state is given compressed expression in the line "I heard a bustling rumor like a fray;" "rumor" has the special Elizabethan sense of noise as well as the general meaning of uncertain and possibly dangerous news, and both meanings are present here; they suggest to Portia the word "fray," or battle as her mind moves automatically from any noise she hears to the violence she knows is impending. Shakespeare adds to Plutarch the dialogue between Portia and the soothsayer. Since he has predicted Caesar's death on this very day, his appearance heightens Portia's anxiety, and our own expectancy. Will he reach Caesar? With the soothsayer's apparently innocent remark that the "throng . . ./Will crowd a feeble man almost to death" we may imagine Portia's almost uncontrollable alarm as she envisions what deaths may be at that moment occurring. Plutarch records that Portia "swooned:" Shakespeare turns this bare fact into dramatic dialogue in Portia's last speech. It is in ironic contrast to her proven ability (Act II, Sc. 1, 300) to sustain pain on her own account.

ACT III · SCENE 1

Summary

The scene is the street just outside the open Senate house. The Senate can be seen assembled. Caesar, accompanied by Antony, Lepidus and two senators as well as the conspirators, enters, passing through the crowd-lined street where the soothsayer and Artemidorus are waiting.

Fate now gives Caesar two more chances, which increase the suspense in the audience still further. Caesar notices the soothsayer and, remembering his warning, remarks rather that the Ides of March have come. The soothsayer answers meaningfully that they have not come yet. Artemidorus immediately hands Caesar his list of the conspirators. Decius is quick to step ahead of him to present a petition from Trebonius. Artemidorus, in despair, calls out to Caesar to read his first because it is very important to him personally. He has said the wrong thing to Caesar in his present mood, for Caesar tucks it away to be considered later and says he will deal with other people's business before he deals with his own. Artemidorus gives one more agonized request that he read the paper instantly, and arouses Caesar's anger, of which Cassius takes advantage to cut Artemidorus off until after they get to the Capitol.

The procession moves on to the Senate chamber. Popilius, the senator, gives the conspirators a start by whispering to Cassius that he wishes him luck. They think their plot is discovered and Cassius decides to commit suicide on the spot if it is. Popilius has only been teasing them, however, for though he speaks to Caesar it is evident he is not revealing anything, for

Caesar is smiling. The conspirators now go into action according to plan. Trebonius draws Mark Antony outside where he will be unable to interfere with the assassination. Metellus Cimber, with exaggerated humility, kneels to present a feather to Caesar, who, thinking that it is for the cancellation of his brother's banishment, and disgusted at this un-Roman show of humility, rudely and arrogantly refuses to alter the decree. Metellus, as part of the plan, calls in the others. Brutus, Cassius and Casca crowd in, each reinforcing Metellus Cimber's appeal. They are even more arrogantly refused. Then Casca, in seeming desperation, strikes the first dagger-blow at the back of Caesar's neck. He bungles his aim through excitement, but the others press in and repeatedly stab Caesar, who, when he sees Brutus among them, ceases to resist, and takes the blows.

As Caesar dies, Cinna and Cassius let out hysterical cries about liberty and freedom but there does not seem to be any definite plan of action for the next step. Apparently, the conspirators thought the senators would remain transfixed with horror or rejoicing in their seats. Brutus makes a futile attempt to keep them there so he can address them, but they have been tumbling over one another to get outside and away, and the only one he can find to reassure is the aged Publius. Trebonius reports Antony has fled to his house, "amazed."

The conspirators expect to be attacked and, in the meantime, bolster their consciences and courage with high-flying words, theatrically foreshadowing their eternal fame as liberators.

Mark Antony's servant enters to present his respects, assure them of his good will and request that Antony be safely conducted to the conspirators to learn why Caesar deserved this fate. Brutus sends a verbal safe-conduct. Cassius has grave misgivings about this, but Brutus is certain Antony can be retained as a friend.

Antony appears and, making no attempt to conceal his grief, addresses Caesar's body, and tells the conspirators that if they intend to kill him there can be no place or time more fit than here and now. Brutus reassures him, and Cassius seconds Brutus. Brutus promises Antony a full explanation later when the people have been quieted and, Antony, somewhat ironically, shakes their hands all around as a bond of friendship, and explains his delicate position. They must look upon him either as a coward or a flatterer. From these words he goes into a eulogy on Caesar which ends with the subtle comparison of Caesar and a deer driven to bay and pulled down by a pack of dogs.

Cassius is business-like. He interrupts Antony to ask what he intends to do. Will he be enrolled among their friends or shall they proceed without him? Antony replies that he will be their friend when they have given him their reasons for this deed. They promise to do so, and Antony requests to be allowed to speak at Caesar's funeral. Cassius objects, but Brutus overrules him and makes his fourth and most serious mistake. Brutus poses conditions for Antony's speaking: first, Brutus will speak before he does; second, he will not blame the conspirators; third, he will speak all the good he can of Caesar; fourth, he will make the point that he is speaking with the conspirators' permission; and fifth, he will speak from the same platform as Brutus does. Antony accepts. The conspirators leave. Antony, alone with Caesar's body, addresses it in an eloquent speech, an earnest indication of what he will do later in the Forum, and asks pardon for his seeming approval of these murderers' bloody deed.

A servant of Octavius Caesar arrives to say that his master is only twenty miles out of Rome. Antony sends him back to tell his master that Rome is not safe for him yet and to stay where he is. On second thought he detains the servant to hear his speech in the Forum and then carry the news to his master. He bids him help remove the body of Caesar.

Commentary

This, the assassination scene, is the central or pivotal scene of the play. All that has gone before leads up to it as a climax, and it provides the motives and impetus for the second half of the play. It is a highly theatrical scene, and we must visualize the action carefully. Caesar enters and moves toward the center of the stage. The soothsayer and Artemidorus struggle to get near Caesar with their warnings but they are crowded aside, mainly by Decius and Cassius. At the Capitol we have two groups on the stage: Caesar is the center of one, and the conspirators form the other. As the dialogue continues, the second group moves slowly to surround and infiltrate the first, loosening the daggers beneath their togas. The tension increases further with Popilius Lena's ambiguous remark to Cassius (Act III, Sc. 1, 13). Shakespeare takes this detail from Plutarch, who goes on to say that the conspirators "were afraid, every man of them, and looked in one another's face," which further suggests to Shakespeare the tense, frightened exchange between Brutus and Cassius which follows.

Caesar's speeches as the conspirators close in on him are in his most arrogant vein. The phrase "preordinance and first decree" which he associates with his own inflexibility are more properly applied to divine or superhuman laws. He is also the "Northern Star," pre-eminent in the heavens, and "Olympus," home of the gods. The petitioners surrounding him are, on the other hand, first compared to flatterers given to "Low-crooked curtsies," next to fawning spaniels and finally to curs whom Caesar kicks aside. The dictator's view of himself as a god has never been more in evidence. A curious detail in the history of Shakespeare criticism is relevant here. Shakespeare's great fellow-dramatist, Ben Jonson, remarked that at this point in the play Shakespeare shows us Caesar replying to a subject with the line "Caesar never did wrong, but with just cause" which, Jonson adds, was "ridiculous." Jonson's prestige as a critic was great, and presumably it caused Shakespeare to remove the line, since the Folio edition of 1623 has instead the lines "Know, Caesar doth not wrong, nor without cause/Will he be satisfied." The substitution is unfortunate; the lines are weak, and in fact make little sense in the context. Shakespeare's original version (if Jonson recalls it correctly, and there is no reason to doubt him) was far better. Caesar's illogicality, which Jonson presumably objected to, is exactly the sort of thing that a leader, obsessed with his own greatness, and believing himself to be inevitably in the right, might say. It is the dictator's habit of thought that George Orwell has called "doublethink," and it is quite in accord with everything else Caesar says of himself. Shakespeare, or, as we should prefer to think, the editors of the Folio, have removed a minor but telling detail of characterization from the play.

Returning to our visualization of the action on the stage, we have Caesar elaborating on his own greatness and the conspirators, now grouped tightly around him, in poses of humility. This last detail is important and Shakespeare emphasizes it. Metellus is already on his knees. Cassius, after pleading for Caesar's pardon, falls "As low as to thy foot." Cinna and Decius set up a chorus of "O Caesar, Great Caesar." Their fawning is as exaggerated as Caesar's pride. On the stage, this servility will come out even more strongly than in the text, and gives to the audience a sense of hypocrisy and betrayal that is made emphatic by Casca's movement, as he circles behind Caesar to strike the first blow. Shakespeare again refuses to oversimplify his presentation. Caesar may be a tyrant, but he is also stabbed in the back. The conspirators may be convinced of the rightness of their cause, but cold-blooded murder, operating under the guise of flattery, cannot appear in action as anything but vicious, whatever the reasons. It is said that after Caesar saw Brutus among the conspirators he muffled his head in his toga and ceased to defend himself. On the stage, Caesar's recognition of his friend, and the accompanying gesture of hopeless resignation, is particularly effective. We may not be moved to pity for Caesar, but we do recognize the pathos of Brutus, obliged to kill his friend for his principles.

After the assassination, chaos follows, represented by the kind of general noise and movement taking place on the stage. Brutus stands firm in the midst of this. He restrains his followers, comforts an elderly and frightened senator, and publicly announces the conspirators' assumption of responsibility for what they have done. Cassius, always aware of the practical, checks on the whereabouts of Antony. In this whirl of talk, of suggestion and counter-suggestion, it becomes clear that the conspirators have no real notion of what it is they want to do. Even Brutus indicates that whatever develops will be a matter of chance. Later we shall be able to compare this undirected enthusiasm to the astute planning of Antony and Octavius.

It is Brutus who suggests the ceremony of washing hands in the blood of Caesar. It is reminiscent of a sacrificial ritual, and we recall the manner in which Brutus earlier viewed the killing (Act II, Sc. 1, 162-183) as a religious rite, and the conspirators as "purgers" rather than "murderers." Here again Brutus is anxious that others see him (and that he see himself) in a morally acceptable role, performing a duty to the state. However, at this point there is, perhaps, some irony in the pretence of the 'religious sacrifice' of Caesar.

This will be particularly true on the stage, where the blood provides a silent comment (stage blood was common in the Elizabethan theater). Through Brutus' speech Shakespeare carefully indicates that the conspirators are ''Up to the elbows'' in blood and wave their ''red weapons'' over their heads. The bloodstained evidence of murder will make an ironic contrast in the audience's mind with the cries of ''Peace, freedom, liberty!''

Some critics have seen the entrance of Antony's servant as the turning point of the play. There is no need to try to be exact about the precise point. What is certain is that the arrival of Antony on the scene does change the general movement or direction of the action, since he is the nemesis (avenging spirit) of the conspirators. The rest of the play is concerned with their defeat and death. Another result of this change in the course of the action is a change in the relationship of the characters. Characters in drama are usually defined by contrast with one another, rather like colors in a painting. Until now there has been a marked contrast between Brutus and Cassius. We have seen a Cassius who is hard-headed, politically astute, a realist who will take any means to further his ends. He was drawn in sharp contrast to Brutus, whose outstanding characteristics have been (and remain) his high-mindedness, moral concern for the general good of Rome, and a lack of the practical sense and shrewd (and often selfish) judgment needed in a political rebellion. Cassius provided a foil, or contrast, to Brutus, and Brutus' character stood out more clearly because of Cassius. With Antony assuming a major role in the play, it is now he who provides the contrast to Brutus, rather than Cassius. This contrast is most dramatically evident, of course, in the scene containing the two men's funeral speeches over Caesar. Cassius, on the other hand, ceases to be contrasted to Brutus in the second half of the play and becomes simply his partner in misfortune.

It is significant that Antony sends his servant to the conspirators before arriving himself. He must make sure the ground is safe, and the servant's speech is a carefully prearranged one, in which Antony manages to convey the idea that both Brutus and Caesar are heroes, that he loves them both, and that as he was loyal to Caesar, so will he be able to be loyal to Brutus. What Antony wants is a guarantee of safety until he can put his plans in motion, and this he gets at once from Brutus.

Antony enters almost immediately after his servant, and everything he says in public, from here until the end of his funeral speech, is calculated with extreme cunning to reduce suspicion, and to confirm Brutus' notion that he is straightforward, no schemer, and basically harmless. Cassius has his suspicions, but Antony knows that Brutus is the leader, and it is to Brutus that he directs his performance. First he sets to work on Brutus' well-known honesty and integrity. For Brutus, personal betrayal, the desertion of a friend in danger or death would be a moral failing of the first order; therefore Antony begins with a display of grief at the sight of Caesar's body. This is not to say that Antony is being hypocritical. We may assume his deep feeling for Caesar; what is important here is his ability to make tactical use of this feeling. The honest show of grief for the lost friend and the lost cause is exactly the sort of loyalty that will appeal to Brutus. He then does just what Brutus might have done in the same position: offers himself as a victim beside the body of his friend and ruler: "here by Caesar, and by you cut off." It is a shrewd move because it forces the conspirators to assure him of his safety, and of their good will toward him — "With all kind love, good thoughts, and reverence." This is Brutus speaking, but notice Cassius' reply to Antony; Cassius is suspicious of Antony, as one political manipulator of another. He disregards the expression of grief and loyalty, and makes what is, quite simply, an offer of a share of the proceeds and powers issuing from Caesar's death. Antony, with his eye on the incorruptible Brutus, is careful to overlook this offer.

Antony has not only preserved his life and freedom of action, he has won Brutus' support, and he can now afford to enlarge his role a little. He makes an elaborate show of shaking the hand of each of the assassins in turn. It is not until Act V, Sc. 1 that the savage irony with which Antony plays his part comes home. The "Gentlemen all" of this speech there become, in Antony's words, the murderers who "showed your teeth like apes, and fawned like hounds," and "my valiant Casca" here will then be called "damned Casca" who "like a cur, behind, struck Caesar on the neck."

Antony has one more task — a practical one — and he accomplishes it when he asks for "reasons" for the killing and, assured by Brutus that he will hear them, he adds another request, as an innocent afterthought: might he "moreover" speak at Caesar's funeral, "as becomes a friend?" And, of course, Brutus agrees.

In the following debate between Cassius and Brutus (held in asides) it is clear that Cassius is still the practical thinker of the conspiracy but that Brutus, the moral mainstay and public leader, can overrule him (as he does also in Act II, Sc. 1, 114 ff.). Brutus' argument here is interesting because it reveals both his lack of astuteness as far as other people are concerned — after Antony's honest performance, he refuses to suspect him — and his naïve certainty that his own cause, because it is right, need only be put to the people to convince them. "I will myself into the pulpit first/And show the reason of our Caesar's death" seems to him a sufficient answer to Cassius' doubts.

The conspirators leave the stage to Antony, and his violent outburst gives some indication of the strain under which he has been laboring. With them his language had been careful and controlled in accordance with the effects he wished to produce. Here we have naked, undisguised grief, hatred, and an impassioned desire for revenge. The "gentlemen" become "these butchers," and Antony moves on from them to the notion of the general slaughter which will result from Caesar's death. The ghost seeking revenge was a familiar and sinister figure on the Elizabethan stage, and Antony conjures it up here for the audience with "Caesar's spirit, ranging for revenge . . . come(s) hot from hell." But this is more than a figure of speech, or reference to the stage convention of the revenger. There are, in fact, two Caesars in the play: the man the conspirators have killed and the "spirit" who haunts the rest of the play, and whose effect we shall see in Acts IV and V. Antony's speech here, with its predictions concerning "Domestic fury and fierce civil strife," confirm the power of this second Caesar. Shakespeare also solved a technical problem with Antony's speech. Throughout the play thus far our concentration has been on the events leading to the murder of Caesar. Now that Caesar is dead there would be an inevitable relaxation in dramatic pressure, if not for the force of Antony's speech here and its anticipation of new crises to come. Of course, in the theater we would never realize that Shakespeare had 'a dramatic problem' at this point, simply because he solves it so neatly.

ACT III · SCENE 2

Summary

Brutus and Cassius appear in the Forum which is more lively than usual with an excited populace to whom Julius Caesar was a beloved benefactor and hero. They are angrily demanding an explanation of his death. Brutus considers it wise to split up the mob between himself and Cassius to assist their hearing and to keep the masses as small as possible. So the people divide, and Brutus begins his speech in his dry, formal style, purposely appealing to reason and avoiding stirring the emotions. Historically, this was Brutus' style of public speaking, commonly called laconic, or Spartan. His great reputation for uprightness and his dignified presence get him a hearing and replies when he asks for them. He tells them his love for Caesar was as great as any friend's of Caesar's was, but that he loved Rome and the freedom of her citizens more and, because Caesar was ambitious and about to make all Romans slaves, it was necessary to remove him.

The citizens are impressed and they shout for him as a deliverer, and they want to honor him by forming a noisy procession and conducting him home. He puts a damper on their enthusiasm by telling them to let him alone and to stay to hear Mark Antony who speaks with his permission.

Antony starts speaking to a mildly hostile crowd still remembering something of what Brutus has said. He surprises them from the first by his humility and reasonableness. He describes the assassins as noble and honorable men and repeats that word honorable until the ironic use he is making of it has sunk consciously or unconsciously into the very system of his hearers. His insistence on the words ambition and ambitious is in the same vein and to the same effect. Accomplished actor that he is, he allows the crowd to see him apparently overcome with grief for his friend Caesar. Such emotion is infectious. He knows now he has them. Their comments during his pause for effect assure him they are with him now. It remains only for him to excite them to anger.

He goes about it systematically, using every device known to oratory — irony, passion, flattery, ridicule, and finally appeal to self-interest and material betterment. He displays a document which he says is Caesar's will, which has made provision for them; but he must not read it to them. They shout to have it read. He puts them off to arouse their curiosity. He flatters them, and when they again demand the will, he comes down from the platform and, rising to his highest pitch of emotional appeal, shows them the bloody, mutilated body of Caesar, reminds them, by pointing to the bloody mantle on the body, of Caesar's greatest military triumphs, which all Romans more or less felt a share in, and finally connects the individual assassins with the various holes in the cloak. This is all pure acting, both the identification of the cloak and identification of the holes in it — quite unscrupulous, purposeful acting.

Now that he has suggested mutiny sufficiently to make his hearers think of mob action, and has roused their passion, he appeals to their self-interest and personal gratitude. The time has come to read the will. He tells them briefly that Caesar has left each man a legacy of seventy-five drachmas, and for their public use, all his famous gardens across the Tiber surrounding that villa of his where Cleopatra had been living for the last two years, and from which she was even at the moment fleeing home to Egypt.

Thoroughly agitated now, the crowd has become a mob. They seize benches, chairs, anything wooden from the buildings around, heap them high, place Caesar's body on this pyre and snatch lighted torches from the pile with which they rush to set fire to the assassin's houses.

Antony, thoroughly satisfied with a job well done, remarks to himself, "Now let it work." A servant enters to tell him Octavius is in Rome, with Lepidus, at Caesar's house, waiting for him. He goes with the servant.

Commentary

In this scene Antony's power is made clear, and it is a power which works, not through physical violence, but verbal persuasion. This point is important to the play as a whole. *Julius Caesar* is a political play in the broadest sense of that term: it deals with the way men achieve power, and the attempt to justify their actions to others, and to society. A large part of the first half of the play is concerned with persuasion, the ways in which people can be convinced, by honest or dishonest argument, that they ought to act in a certain way. Notice how many occasions we have had, up to this point, to watch people being 'talked into' something. The tribunes convince the people that they ought not to celebrate Caesar's triumph; Cassius convinces Brutus that Caesar ought to be destroyed; Portia convinces Brutus that he ought to tell her of his plans; Calphurnia convinces Caesar that he ought not to go to the Capitol, and Decius convinces him that he must go. This scene is wholly constructed of two opposing arguments: Brutus' defence of Caesar's assassination, and Antony's attack of it. The scene is important, not simply because of its contribution to the plot, but because it also deals with one of the main issues, or questions, of the play: how do people act, when confronted with a vital public or political decision? On the basis of this scene the answer is that their actions are far from rational, and that they can be directed at will by anyone who, like Antony, can manipulate an audience with his words.

The funeral speech, or *laudatio funebris*, was a common Roman custom. Plutarch mentions it in connection with Caesar's death, but he gives no account of what was said. Shakespeare invents both speeches, and makes them into a brilliant contrast. Everything about the two speakers — their characters, political attitudes, strengths and weaknesses — is implied in what they say.

Brutus speaks in prose, a form which suits the sober, orderly presentation of what he has to say. His calm, factual and colorless delivery is in direct contrast with the poetry of Antony. Brutus' opening remarks ("Be patient till the last . . . be silent, that you may hear") have the quality of a teacher rapping for the attention of his class, and what he says is very like a lecture. The construction of the speech is careful and controlled. Notice, for example, the continual use of parallel constructions (e.g., loved-weep, fortunate-rejoice, valiant-honor, ambitious-slew). This sort of arrangement has the effect of rational, logical development, almost like a mathematical demonstration, and Brutus' "I pause for a reply" at the end of the passage is a mark of confidence. Brutus has made two vital errors of judgment in this speech, and both of them stem (as all his errors do) from qualities which we admire. In the first place he has assumed that, since his cause is just, it needs only to be presented to be believed. It is one of his fundamental beliefs that justice and truth will prevail in this world, and it is shown to be a naïve one. His second mistake is to assume that others, like himself, will be persuaded by reason. The qualities of the crowd that Antony works on so effectively — emotion, uncertainty, greed — are not understood by Brutus. One of the great defects of his virtue is to assume the existence of the same virtue in everyone else. Brutus' dangerous lack of insight into the practical realities of persuasion and the mob-mind is further revealed in his complete misunderstanding of the reaction to his speech. He has demonstrated with clarity and precision why the death of Caesar, or of any tyrant who wants to be a Caesar, is necessary. The crowd's acclaim shows how little they have understood him. The shout of "Let him be Caesar" is an effective comment on their ignorance of the real issues involved. Yet Brutus does not see that a crowd which can acclaim him for all the wrong reasons is also one which can be totally reworked by Antony. Innocently confident of the justice and success of his own cause, Brutus leaves the speaking platform to his adversary.

Antony's speech has been generally considered one of Shakespeare's most brilliant creations. Sir Harley Granville-Barker comments:

> the cheapening of the truth, the appeals to passion, the perfect
> carillon of flattery, cajoling, mockery and pathos, swinging to a
> magnificent tune, all serve make it a model of what popular oratory

should be. In a school for demagogues its critical analysis might well be an item on every examination paper.

In fact, Antony's political oratory is such that audiences are often taken in by it. As in the preceding scene, Antony's emotion is genuine; it is the subtle manipulation of the audience which lies beneath the apparent artlessness of the speech that is so clever.

When Antony takes the stand his audience is clearly pro-Brutus and he guides himself accordingly. He denies any intention of praising Caesar, and refers to the "noble" Brutus. There is, however, a slight double edge at the mention of Caesar's ambition — "If it were so." Antony is careful not to proceed too rapidly, and the phrase "Honorable man" is delivered in a straightforward manner. The word "honorable" recurs in the speech like a refrain. It is used eight times, each time with increasing bitterness, and finally in open contempt. Actors who play Antony often make the mistake of making Antony say the word sarcastically at the very outset of the speech; but Antony waits until the crowd is itself ready to give the word a savage twist — "They were traitors. Honorable men!"

Antony's manipulation of his hearers falls into several phases. First he deals with the question of Caesar's ambition, carefully slanting his remarks so they will appeal to i) the people's poverty — Caesar filled the "general coffers," and "wept" when the poor were unhappy, and ii) their sense of their own importance: they would all recall that it was at their insistence that Caesar refused the crown offered to him at the feast of Lupercal. Next, Antony suggests that, in refusing to mourn Caesar, "men have lost their reason." This may be too directly critical at this stage, so he shifts their attention with a display of his own emotion. Antony's point is made. The citizens see that "there is much reason" in what he says (heavily ironic, when one remembers the genuinely reasonable speech by Brutus) and are also affected by his grief. Next Antony uses the rhetorical device of introducing an idea which he wishes his audience to take up by pretending to deny it. To move the crowd "to mutiny and rage" would be to do wrong to the conspirators, and he would rather "wrong the dead . . . and you." It is a subtle touch, and suggests to the listeners that they are on Caesar's side, that they have been wronged, and that "mutiny and rage" may be in order. Thus far Antony has used innuendo and implication; it is time for something tangible and solid, and he introduces Caesar's will. Where a less skillful orator would certainly proceed, at this climax, to capitalize on the introduction of the will by reading it, Antony holds back. Instead he works on his audience's boundless suggestibility by telling them what they will feel when they do hear it, unless they are "wood" or "stones." Now Antony descends to Caesar's body; by this point he is in complete control, and he orders and arranges the crowd at will. It is time for more tangible evidence, now of a direct and visual kind, and Antony refers to the blood-stained "rents" in Caesar's toga, ending with the wound inflicted by "well-beloved" Brutus.

Antony can now risk open encouragement to violence against the "blood treason" he has revealed. If he were an able speaker, he says (with an irony lost on his hearers), he would move "The stones of Rome to rise and mutiny." This is enough for the mob, but as they set off to find the conspirators, Antony calls them back. He has worked his will on them, and he can now afford to point out with something close to amused contempt (which they, of course, miss) the senselessness of the passions he has aroused — "you go to do you know not what." They have forgotten the will. Antony is clever enough to know that, while a group will act violently and immediately on the basis of a powerful shared emotion, something further is needed to motivate the individual when the group-emotion has passed. Therefore he ends his speech with a specific appeal to the greed of each of them: Caesar's bequest of the "walks, arbors, orchards" and to "every several man, seventy-five drachmas." And only then is he content to let them go.

ACT III · SCENE 3

Summary

This is the mob in action with all its unreasoning fury. Cinna, a poet and friend of Caesar's, having had a disturbing dream of refusing a dinner invitation of Caesar's and being compelled by Caesar to go, goes into the streets to watch Caesar's funeral. The mob discovers his name is Cinna, also the name of one of the conspirators, and though he protests desperately that he is another Cinna, a poet, they tear him limb from limb anyway. Then they rush off to burn the houses of Brutus, Cassius, Decius, Casca and Ligarius.

Commentary

The purpose of this scene is to dramatize, in one brief, violent incident, the result of Antony's speech. The first act of the mob, their emotions excited and their reason obscured, is the senseless murder of an innocent man. The mob mistakes Cinna the poet for Cinna the conspirator; yet even when he tells them their mistake, they butcher him anyway "for his bad verses." There is a curious irony in the fact that the man whose life was devoted to the perceptive and sensitive use of language should be the victim of a totally different way of using language — to produce rage, hatred, and destructive hysteria.

Shakespeare's handling of this mob scene and some others like it (notably in *Coriolanus*) has caused some critics to say that he distrusted and even hated the ordinary people. This judgment is based on a misunderstanding of the way Shakespeare treats 'the people' in his plays. In this play, for example, we are given a group of "commoners" in the opening scene, but they are not a 'mob.' They are rather a collection of individuals — carpenters and cobblers — and indeed they contribute the only comic role in the play: the amiable cobbler who outwits the tribunes. If we compare them to the crowd in Act III, Sc. 2 and 3, we see the difference. In the latter scenes there are no individuals, only a mob, swayed by mob-emotions. What they say is neither individual nor witty, as in the case of the cobbler, but a generalized, undifferentiated shout of violence — "Tear him, tear him! Come, brands ho! firebrands!" We meet a great many 'ordinary people' in Shakespeare — bright and stupid, sweet and sour, proper and improper — and they are all, in their way, attractive. But we never meet an attractive mob.

ACT IV · SCENE 1

Summary

It does not matter that historically the events of this scene occurred more than a year after the events of the last. Unity of theme and action was all that Shakespeare usually cared for.

The triumvirs who now rule Rome and Italy (Antony, Octavius and Lepidus) are making up their notorious list of persons who are to be placed outside the protection of the law and whom anyone may kill. Each puts down the names of people he dislikes most, and these include Lepidus' brother and Antony's nephew (really it was his uncle), with the consent of Lepidus and Antony in each case. It is a shameless bargaining of lives.

Lepidus, who is a first-class general but not an influential politician, is sent off by Antony to Caesar's house to fetch Caesar's will so that they can do some distributing of Caesar's legacy to the poor. While he is gone Antony complains to Octavius about Lepidus' futility as one of their number, saying he is a man fit only to be sent on errands for the other two. Octavius defends him as a splendid soldier, remembering, no doubt, his military record and that he was a close friend of Julius Caesar. This does not impress Antony who intends to use him as a tool and then fling him away.

We then learn that Brutus and Cassius are recruiting armies and are about to threaten the position in Rome of the triumvirs. The three rulers must arrange to meet this challenge. Octavius reveals that their position is dangerous, since they are surrounded by enemies, and there are a host of false friends in their midst.

Commentary

In Act III, Sc. 3 we witnessed the public result of Antony's victory: mindless brutality. In this scene we are shown the result at a higher political level: the deliberate, cold-blooded imposition of the death sentence on a long list of Romans. Plutarch's version is as follows:

> They could hardly agree whom they would put to death: for every one of them would kill their enemies and save their kinsmen and friends. Yet at length, giving place to their greedy desire to be revenged of their enemies, they spurned all reverence of blood and holiness of friendship at their feet... they condemned three hundred of the chiefest citizens of Rome to be put to death by proscription.

Antony's opening line, which is particularly effective because of the contrast between its flat, unemotional tone and its subject, sets the mood. There follows a grisly piece of relative-trading between Antony and Lepidus, and then Antony's announcement that he has no intention (and possibly never did have any intention) of fulfilling the promises in Caesar's will, which he had used so effectively to enrage the mob against the conspirators. Although he is only mentioned in passing, the spirit of Brutus is powerfully present throughout this scene. We are seeing the result of his earnest, selfless attempt to save Rome from tyranny. In the world of practical politics, his effort has resulted in the dictatorship of the triumvirate of Antony, Octavius and Lepidus, and we are left in no doubt about the nature of their rule: it is cynical, bloody and absolute. The relations between the three are also significant. Antony and Octavius are wary of each other, as well they might be. Their open rivalry will be the subject of another play, Antony and Cleopatra. Antony's dismissal of Lepidus indicates that the triumvirate has nothing to do with friendship or principle. It is a naked struggle for power, in which Lepidus is just a "property." The long analogy made between Lepidus and a beast of burden also illuminates Antony's view of his fellow men: they are to be used, as he used the mob, like animals.

ACT IV · SCENE 2

Summary

This short scene introduces us to the camps of the conspirators. Brutus and Cassius are in command of the armies which they have recruited separately in the various Roman provinces and kingdoms of Asia Minor. They are joining forces at Sardis on their way to meet Antony and Octavius, who are advancing across Macedonia eastward. Events in the Roman world have come to a crisis, and this time there is to be a "show-down."

Brutus halts his army. His officer Lucilius is returning from a visit to Cassius' approaching army. He brings a letter and is accompanied by Pindarus, a servant of Cassius. Brutus reads the letter and then makes the unpardonable mistake of criticizing Cassius in front of his own servant, who loyally but courteously supports his master. Brutus makes a further mistake of asking his own officer, Lucilius, about his reception by Cassius, and then criticizing him in front of Lucilius. These lapses are not only unwise, but serious breaches of military etiquette in any age or army.

Lucilius says Cassius is close at hand, and he shortly appears. Without waiting to greet or receive greeting, Cassius, who is very angry, accuses Brutus on sight of having done him wrong. Brutus invites Cassius into his tent so that they shall not be seen quarrelling in front of their two armies. The armies are led away, and Brutus and Cassius enter the tent.

Commentary

The remaining action of the play concerns the defeat and deaths of

Brutus and Cassius. The scene is no longer Rome. Brutus and Cassius have gone to the east to collect troops. The scene moves accordingly, first to the camp of Brutus near Sardis, in Asia Minor, and then to the plain of Philippi in Macedonia, where the final battle is fought. The scene change makes little difference, of course, on the Elizabethan stage; we need concern ourselves only with the characters and the poetry.

Act IV, Sc. 2 begins the famous 'quarrel scene' between Brutus and Cassius, which runs through to Act IV, Sc. 3, where their reconciliation is sealed with drink of wine. The division between the two scenes is the invention of 18th-century editors, and we may ignore it except for purposes of line reference. The division between the two leaders on which this scene is based is recounted by Plutarch as follows:

> Brutus sent to pray Cassius to come to the city of Sardis, and went to meet him . . . . Now, as it commonly happeneth in great affairs between two persons, both of them having many friends, and so many captains under them, there ran tales and complaints between them. Therefore they went into a little chamber together, and bade every man avoid, and did shut the doors to them.

ACT IV · SCENE 3

Summary

This, the quarrel scene, is perhaps the most famous single scene in Shakespeare's plays. It ranges in tone from cold fury, through hot anger, to scorn and defiance and threat, and eventually ends up a reassertion of warm friendship and, at last, cool calculations for strategic battle action.

Cassius accuses Brutus of punishing a friend of his for taking bribes in Sardis in spite of Cassius' representations on his behalf. Brutus insists that the guilty should be punished; that is what they killed Caesar for: that justice might survive. Brutus charges Cassius with unjust methods of raising money from the people of the country, but in almost the same breath accuses him of refusing to send him some of that very money to pay his troops. With Brutus coldly indifferent to Cassius' violent threats, Cassius' old admiration and love finally get the better of him and he breaks down in misery because Brutus has lost all affection for him. This brings Brutus quickly around, and they make up their differences and are back on their former footing of deep friendship, perhaps a footing of deeper friendship. Brutus, to answer Cassius' criticism about being unable to bear his misfortunes, mentions that Portia is dead, having committed suicide by swallowing live coals. Cassius is astonished at Brutus' self-command. A meddling pseudo-philosopher forces himself in, in spite of the sentries, to get the generals to make up. They both turn on him and turn him out. Then, with their officers, they plan future action. Once more Brutus overrules Cassius and makes his last big mistake, insisting that they advance across the Dardanelles to Macedonia and meet Antony and Octavius at Philippi. Cassius and the others leave.

Left alone, Brutus sits down to read while his boy, Lucius, plays to him for a moment or two till he falls asleep. Just then the ghost of Caesar appears to Brutus and promises to meet him at Philippi. Brutus awakens Lucius and his two sentries, but though they cry out in their sleep they cannot remember having dreamed anything.

Commentary

In Plutarch the actual quarrel between Cassius and Brutus takes very little space, but Shakespeare makes a good deal of it. Plutarch says that "they began to pour out their complaints one to the other, and grew hot and loud, earnestly accusing one another, and at length both fell a-weeping." Shakespeare's version has received a great deal of praise, and some unfavorable criticism. As early as 1692 Thomas Rymer wrote that the two generals resembled "two drunken Hectors huffing and swaggering for a two-penny reckoning," but Rymer wrote in an age when tragic figures were obliged to maintain an inflexible nobility at all times. Other critics, notably Bradley, have said that the incident is dramatically irrelevant. This is true only if one considers the play as a chain of historical events, or a plot-sequence. The fact that so many critics have found it powerful and that audiences are always moved by it indicates that it is necessary to the development and total imaginative effect of the play. Coleridge went so far as to say that he "knew of no part of Shakespeare" that so impressed him "with the belief of his genius being superhuman."

The subject of the argument appears as soon as the two leaders are alone within the tent. Bribes have been taken from the local Sardians, and Cassius himself is suspected of having "an itching palm" in this respect. This criticism, coming from Brutus, has a twofold power. We may well imagine his attitude to the practice of taking bribes in general, and the righteous scorn in the phrase "sell and mart your offices for gold." But Brutus has another, deeper source of concern, and he goes on to make an indirect reference to it. We recall Brutus' anguish over the morality involved in joining the conspiracy against Caesar (Act II, Sc. 1). There he was worried about his own motives and honesty. More recently he has been given a painful lesson, by Antony, of the way in which professed and actual motives may differ — of the dishonesty, in short, that surrounds the struggle for power. Is the conspiracy on which he has staked his moral being itself corrupt? He uses the word when he remarks "The name of Cassius honors this corruption," and goes on to address not only Cassius, but himself. His anger and the desperate, questioning quality of the speech indicate that Brutus is thinking of the moral basis of the whole enterprise, as well as the particular lapse on Cassius' part: "Did not great Julius bleed for justice sake?" and "shall we not/Contaminate our fingers . . . sell the mighty space of our large honors?" Cassius, however, pays no attention to this line of moral self-examination. For him the attack is personal, and he rapidly brings the argument to the level of direct insult. He is, he says, the "older" and "abler" soldier: "You are not . . . I am . . . I say you are not . . . Urge me no more!'' The pathos here lies in the fact that Cassius does not understand the grounds of Brutus' rage, any more than Brutus understands the way in which his contempt (''I'll use you for my mirth'') wounds Cassius.

Since the part of Brutus in the play requires a continued dignity on the part of the actor, this scene is often played in such a way as to make Brutus seem above the conflict. This makes the scene weaker than it might be. Here is the view of one director of the play.

> I would like to decry Brutus' too-often played suprahuman aloof-ness. Far too often, in the quarrel scene, poor Cassius rages in a vacuum while Brutus stand quietly by 'playing' the honest, hon-ourable, loftily Olympian Stoic. This is utter nonsense. Brutus is a human being. He is a powerful, determined crusader who is out-raged at what he considers injustice, further infuriated by the fact that it comes from one he loves deeply, and filled with grief over the death of Portia. The storm breaks, and he flies into a towering rage, showing it with all the vigour and force of a powerful man who has had all he can take . . . at the end Cassius says 'I did not think you would have been so angry,' amazed and shaken at an impassioned scene all the more staggering because it is so rare for Brutus. Both men must play it to the hilt.

It is true that Brutus' righteous anger ought to be given full reign in the scene, but there is another of Brutus' qualities that Shakespeare reminds us of in a minor, subtle touch. Cassius, who is not overly scrupulous about principle, and is carrying out the campaign as forcefully as he can has, apparently, taken funds ''from the hard hands of peasants.'' Brutus would himself be incapable of this kind of extortion. He is ''armed so strong in honesty'' that he ''can raise no money by vile means.'' Yet it turns out that Brutus has asked Cassius for money; although he condemns the extortion, he then asks for some of the profits. Here, as elsewhere, Shakespeare indicates that honor, nobility and integrity are admirable, but that they are often accompanied by self-righteousness and muddleheaded thinking.

We have remarked on how many critics have praised the quarrel scene, although finding it somehow irrelevant to the action as a whole. Bradley remarks on the ''pathos'' of the scene, and says that this is an emotion that frequently occurs somewhere in the second half of a Shakespearean tragedy. There is certainly a pathetic futility in the quarrel. Perhaps the pathos lies mainly in the fact that the two leaders of the conspiracy had, only a few scenes before, been celebrating the ''peace'' they had brought to Rome; now they are engaged in a petty, abusive war with each other. The scene also has the effect of showing us the two men as confused, emotional human beings, rather than as public figures. The supposedly stoical Brutus loses his self-control, and the supposedly selfish Cassius pleads for the love of his friend.

This is not, as some critics have said, a lapse in dignity. It rather brings a new kind of sympathy to bear on the two men.

The reconciliation of the quarrel takes place over a glass of wine and Brutus, in a couple of laconic phrases, reveals the death of Portia. His iron restraint here and later in the scene on the subject of Portia's death is dramatically effective, and adds to what we already know of the man. There are several references throughout the play to Brutus' philosophy. He was a stoic, (as distinct from the epicurian Cassius) but Shakespeare is not particularly concerned with the technical points and assumptions of the stoic philosophy. For him (as for most of us) the chief stoic virtue was strength in the face of suffering, and this required the continual discipline of the emotions. We know of Brutus' love for Portia, and therefore a large element of the dramatic interest in this scene arises from the conflict in him between his love and his self-discipline. Since Brutus does not allow himself to speak of Portia at any length, the actor must suggest the struggle in the way he plays the scene, and some of the drama is lost in reading it. This suggests the solution to a problem that has always troubled scholars and editors at this point in the play. Brutus reveals the death to Cassius and then seems to be ignorant of it later in his talk to Messala. Several ingenious theories have been put forward suggesting that Shakespeare re-wrote the play, adding a second version of the Portia news, and forgetting to remove the first. Scholars and editors have a tendency to think of a Shakespeare play as a document to be read, rather than acted on a stage, and perhaps that has misled them here. Brutus' intense struggle with himself appears first with Cassius, and again with Messala. In the second occurrence he is in public, with his lieutenants, and behaves with the required stoic control — with "meditating" on the possibility of Portia's death he has "the patience to endure it now" — and both Messala and Cassius voice their admiration for his courage. The fact that they do so indicates that the actor playing Brutus reveals an intense, continuing struggle for control, and Shakespeare has put in the two versions to give him the opportunity to do this. It is one of those examples of Shakespeare's stagecraft that we often miss in the printed text.

The visiting soldiers leave and we enter the last phase of this long scene. It begins with a delicate touch, and again, one that is more obvious in the staging than in the reading. Shakespeare frequently writes something like 'stage directions' into his lines — phrases which indicate how the actor should perform. We have one of these in Act IV, Sc. 2, 240; Brutus' "speak'st drowsily" can only mean that Lucius yawns; it is an important detail. Lucius has earlier represented the calm and peace which Brutus, in joining the conspiracy, has lost forever, and here the presence of the sleepy, innocent boy, reminds us again of the other vanished dimension of Brutus' life. This reminder of peace and harmony is expanded in what follows. Brutus' gentleness to the drowsy Lucius, his thoughtfulness in instructing his guards to "sleep on cushions in my tent" is evidence of his civilized humanity, just as the book he takes to read is evidence of his sensitive turn of mind. In fact much of Brutus' misunderstanding of the tactics of the conspiracy, his confident but unwise decisions, his inability to see through Antony's deception, is understandable in the light of this scene. Here we have the scholarly, and in some ways unworldly Brutus on his own. With his soldiers, he has just ordered the preparation for a battle. But on his own he turns to literature and to music.

Music occurs often in Shakespeare's plays. It is, in part, a relief from the strain of dialogue and action, but it has a more important dramatic function. Whether the song is happy or sad, it contributes a powerful emotional sense, or 'atmosphere' to the scene. The song here has an air of melancholy and perhaps nostalgia which underlines this moment of calm.

It is a particularly effective piece of stagecraft to introduce the ghost at this point. For a brief interlude Brutus has been at peace, but the knowledge that he has murdered Caesar, and that the assassination has achieved none of its noble aims, can never be far from him. The ghost's entrance is signified by the candle that "burns ill." This is in accordance with the Elizabethan belief that the appearance of spirits was accompanied by a wind, but it also suggests an effective modern staging. Brutus' reading is interrupted by a gust of wind, and on raising his head he sees the apparition. In the theater of today ghosts, and supernatural occurrences generally, are difficult to manage. Our audiences are accustomed to 'realistic' theater, which shows them only the sort of thing that they expect to see in everyday life. Therefore Shakespeare's ghosts on our stages are usually produced with strange lighting effects or off-stage sounds. This was not a problem for the Elizabethans, who simply accepted ghosts, just as they accepted Macbeth's witches, or his "air-borne dagger." The ghost probably wore a special garment, called "a robe for to go invisible," and he was accepted as being invisible to all those on the stage who were not supposed to see him.

The ghost of Caesar is equally effective whether we imagine it to have objective reality or to be simply a creation of Brutus' exhausted mind. In either case it is a powerful and frightening representation of Caesar, whose presence is felt continually in the last half of the play. It had been the assumption of the conspirators that the death of Caesar would, in itself, produce a new, free Rome. Instead of this, Caesar proved to be more powerful dead than alive. His return to Brutus here is ironic, when we recall Brutus' statement that he wants only to destroy "Caesar's spirit" (Act II, Sc. 1, 169). That is exactly what he has not been able to destroy.

More than in most of Shakespeare's plays, supernatural occurrences and omens abound in *Julius Caesar*. One of the effects of these occurrences is to give us a sense of impending disaster, and that is what the ghost does here. After the brief remembrance of harmony and peace in Lucius' song, Brutus moves towards his final crisis.

ACT V · SCENE 1

Summary

In the manner of medieval times the leaders of the armies hold a parley before engaging in actual fighting. These parleys resulted usually in bitter accusations and the throwing of acid insults across the intervening ground — all of which prepared them for the spirit of battle. This parley runs true to that form. Though Brutus seems willing at the start to consider a compromise, there is no thought of this in the minds of the opposing generals. The parley degenerates into a high-sounding, "mud-slinging" match. Antony charges Brutus and Cassius with the immoral murder of Caesar. Cassius, stung by Antony's words, blames Brutus for not having followed his advice about Antony. Octavius and Antony have to take their position, and Brutus confers apart with Lucilius, his second-in-command, while Cassius confers with Messala. Then follows a noble and touching farewell between Brutus and Cassius, in case they do not see each other again. One gathers that they are highly uncertain as to the outcome of the day. They agree that both will commit suicide on the field rather than be taken prisoner. Altogether, not a bright and promising mood in which to go into battle.

Commentary

The last act of the play concerns the final conflict of the two factions, and here again Shakespeare rearranges and compresses the historical events he found in Plutarch to suit his own dramatic purposes. There were in fact two battles at Philippi; they were separated by about three weeks, and Octavius was not even present at the first. Shakespeare merges the two engagements into a continuous battle, and in this scene he brings Antony and Octavius face to face with Brutus and Cassius in order to contrast the two groups before the struggle begins.

Antony and Octavius appear first, and we are at once impressed with their confidence. Brutus' decision to meet them at Philippi "answers their hopes." It is clear that Brutus has made an error here, and he is to make another (Act V, Sc. 3, 5). Antony seems to have complete knowledge of the enemy intentions, and they are acting, he says, with "fearful bravery," or empty bravado. We are given a strong suggestion here of the desperation in the tactics of Brutus and Cassius, which will be enlarged later in the scene. We have already had sufficient opportunity to observe Antony's ruthless competence in action. Octavius now emerges a little more clearly. There is a minor exchange in which Octavius coolly but firmly asserts his equality to Antony, and later the language he uses to Brutus and Cassius leaves no doubt of his confidence in his own power. It is very possible that Shakespeare, in this subtle strengthening of Octavius' character, is recalling the whole of the Antony-Octavius story as he read it in Plutarch. These two will later struggle for supremacy, with Octavius the victor, and that phase of the story will provide the plot for Antony and Cleopatra. Although Shakespeare waited seven years before writing the later play, he seems to have Octavius' potential power in mind here.

This sort of confrontation between leaders who are about to do battle is common in Shakespeare. Since the battle itself can be given only a restricted presentation on the stage, the hostility is dramatized at length in the dialogue as well. In this debate, we sense an element of weakness or uncertainty in Cassius and Brutus. The sneering comparison of Antony's eloquence to the "honey" and "buzzing" of bees is not very apt in view of what Antony has accomplished. He is a good deal more than a troublesome insect, as Brutus knows. Cassius' phrases calling Octavius and Antony a "schoolboy" and a "reveller" respectively come most inappropriately from a soldier who has been chased from Rome and brought to bay in Macedonia by the two men he here condemns. On the other hand, Antony's denunciation of the conspirators is striking and vivid; we can feel his searing anger. Finally, Octavius' closing words, contemptuously inviting his enemies to fight when they feel they have sufficient courage, have the effect of leaving Brutus and Cassius distinctly at a loss as Octavius and Antony turn their backs on them and stalk off the stage.

The remainder of this scene intensifies our sense of the hopelessness of the cause of Brutus and Cassius. This is done, not by any direct statement, but through a series of suggestive speeches in which the two leaders seem to imply, in spite of themselves, that the end is near. Cassius' violent outburst (after Octavius and Antony have left) has a recklessness about it that is not far from despair. Shakespeare's characters often speak in this way when they feel the trap closing on them (we may recall Macbeth's anguished "Blow wind! Come wrack! At least we'll die with harness on our back!"). The source of Cassius' desperation becomes clearer in the speech to Messala which follows. The "mighty eagles" which had perched on his former ensign would be associated with the bronze eagles which formed the standard of the mighty Roman legions: their power is replaced by the symbol of death in the scavengers ("ravens, crows, and kites"), who traditionally anticipated death. We also recall Cassius' earlier, scornful comment on Caesar's "superstition" (Act II, Sc. 1); now he himself expresses his belief in the "things that do presage."

Both Cassius and Brutus make reference to philosophy in this scene. Cassius' epicurean view held that the mind found its chief virtue in sensible, controlled living (our sense of 'epicurean' came much later), unaffected by any sort of superstition. Brutus' stoic view held that the virtue lay in disciplined endurance. Although Shakespeare has not enlarged on their philosophical principles, he makes both men abandon their philosophies at this point. Cassius forgets his 'rational' rejection of evil signs; he now feels that they predict his death. Brutus the thinker has been opposed to suicide, but Brutus the Roman soldier will refuse to "be led in triumph" as a captive through Rome. Both men have been brooding on the likelihood of their defeat. They do not mention it directly, but this preception of defeat gives deep pathos to the speeches in which they say farewell "for ever and for ever."

ACT V · SCENE 2

Summary
Shakespeare usually meets the difficulty of presenting battle action on the stage by having a series of short scenes, each depicting a small corner of the field and of the action. Brutus sends Messala, who is liaison officer from Cassius' wing, off with messages to bring Cassius' forces in against Antony's wing, for he himself has broken Octavius for the time.

Commentary
There is a brief silence after the farewells of Brutus and Cassius at the end of Scene 1, and then the 'alarum' sounds the battle's beginning. There is often in Shakespeare an alternation between success and failure at the crisis of the play. Here, in Brutus' brief, shouted lines, there seems a momentary chance of victory. Titinius reveals Brutus' error at the beginning of the next scene.

ACT V · SCENE 3

Summary
This scene is a collection of short episodes in the fight. Cassius and Titinius are appraising the field. Cassius has had to take the drastic action of killing his own standard-bearer to prevent a retreat of his wing. Titinius reports that Brutus has given the command too soon, and that his men have defeated Octavius' wing and are plundering his tents, oblivious to the rest of the battle. Pindarus, Cassius' servant, rushes in to urge Cassius to get away quickly or he will be surrounded and taken, for Antony's men are plundering his tents. Cassius gets far enough away for a view and sees his tents on fire and a body of cavalry approaching in the distance. He sends Titinius to find out who they are. Pindarus gets to a higher vantage point to see what happens. He reports that Titinius is surrounded by horsemen and evidently taken prisoner. Cassius gives up hope and forces Pindarus to run him through with his own sword, and the one with which he stabbed Caesar. Pindarus, a captive Parthian, heads for home and is never seen again by the Romans.

It is all a mistake. It was Brutus' troops that surrounded Titinius excitedly telling him of their victory over Octavius' wing. Titinius and Messala find Cassius dead and grieve over the sad misunderstanding that has obviously been the cause of this. When Messala leaves, Titinius stabs himself with Cassius' sword.

Messala brings in Brutus and the others to see Cassius' corpse. The immediate comment of Brutus is much the same as that of Cassius just before he died, that Julius Caesar's spirit is strong and stalking the assassins for vengeance. Grieving, Brutus makes arrangements to have Cassius' body sent to Thasos where his funeral will not dishearten the army, and goes back to take command.

Commentary

This scene exhibits another simple but effective Shakespearean method for representing a battle within the limitations of the Elizabethan stage. Cassius, whose eyesight is "thick" orders Pindarus to the upper stage — representing a point "higher on that hill" — and in their tense exchange we follow the progress of Titinius.

Brutus' glimmer of hope in Scene 2 is seen to be illusory. Cassius' soldiers are defeated by Antony. While Brutus is successful against Octavius he is not able to help Cassius, thus indirectly bringing about Cassius' death. It is ironic that it should be the soldiers of the honest Brutus who "fall to spoil," and, in their looting and plundering, fail to help the forces of Cassius. But it is a further and greater irony that Cassius, who has always perceived the practical realities of the situation around him, is now finally and fatally misled by his servant's report. The presentation of Cassius has changed subtly but drastically in the course of the play, how much so we can see if we recall the soliloquy which closed Act I, Sc. 2. There Cassius, driven by envy and hatred, was a subtle, scheming Machiavellian. But the Cassius of the quarrel scene was a man of dignity, sensitivity, and human warmth. And in a series of details since then (e.g., the belief in omens, the meditation of his birthday, the farewell to Brutus) Shakespeare shows another side to Cassius. This is in part for dramatic reasons. Until the assassination, the unscrupulous Cassius and the honest Brutus were in dramatic contrast; after the assassination the conflict and contrast is largely between Antony and the conspirators. But there is no real inconsistency in Shakespeare's presentation of Cassius. The conspirator of the first half of the play has become the hunted Roman patriot of the second half. Shakespeare simply reveals another aspect of the man, and one which adds pathos to his death. Cassius has predicted before in this play that he will take his own life, and now, as he does, he is able to remark on the irony of the act: Caesar's murderer has become his revenger.

Shakespeare's dramatic concentration of the two battles of Philippi into one leads him into a minor error. Titinius remarks on the setting sun in line 60 and yet Brutus, since another engagement is to come, has to announce that it is three o'clock in the closing lines of the scene. Shakespeare is careless about this kind of detail because it makes no real difference to what he is trying to do on the stage, which is to create a poetic effect.

The pathos of the deaths of Cassius and Titinius is given poetic statement by Brutus. One editor (F.A. Ferguson) says of his closing speech:

> Brutus, however, hopes to live and triumph. The play approaches its climax as does a symphony. The rhythm quickens momentarily, offering a tentative hope of a return to a happier theme. Then chord after chord leads to the tragic close.

ACT V · SCENE 4

Summary

This is another episode in another corner of the field. Brutus, young Cato and Lucilius are closely engaged in hand-to-hand fighting with the enemy. Brutus and Cato get away. Lucilius is taken prisoner and, representing himself as Brutus, tries to convince the enemy soldiers to kill him. They refuse, and Antony, entering, recognizes Lucilius, whom he orders to be well-treated, for he wants him as his friend.

Commentary

This brief scene of battle is a prelude to the final defeat. The action on the stage will be as vigorous and brutal as possible, with Cato's death and Lucilius' capture signifying the final destruction of Brutus' forces. Death is here sought after as an honor, and Lucilius attempts to die in the place of Brutus to show his devotion to him. Shakespeare takes the incident from Plutarch:

> Lucilius seeing a troop of barbarous men going all together right against Brutus, he determined to slay them with the hazard of his life and, being left behind, told them that he was Brutus ... Lucilius was brought to Antonius, and stoutly with a bold countenance said, 'Antonius, I dare assure thee, that no enemy hath taken nor shall take Marcus Brutus alive.'

The scene suggests the loyalty and courage that Brutus inspires. It also contrasts the hopelessness of Brutus' cause with the confident, secure directions with which Antony ends the scene.

ACT V · SCENE 5

Summary

This scene shows us the final stroke of nemesis in the death of Brutus. He is certain now of defeat. He tries to persuade one after another of his men to run him through with a sword but they all refuse. There is an alarm and they all retreat to a safer spot, except Brutus who detains Strato and persuades him to hold his sword. Strato reluctantly consents, and Brutus falls upon his own sword and gives himself a fatal wound. As he dies, once again the fateful words come from his lips, "Caesar, now be still. I killed not thee with half so good a will."

Octavius enters, guided by Messala and Lucilius, both prisoners. They find Brutus' body. Lucilius rejoices that Brutus will not be taken prisoner. Octavius promises to take into his service all who were Brutus' servants, and takes on Strato on the spot.

Antony pronounces a brief but moving eulogy, "This was the noblest

Roman of them all.'' Octavius promises a soldier's funeral; with all honors for Brutus, and they leave the field.

Commentary

Shakespeare takes the details of Brutus' death from Plutarch.

> Now the night being far spent, Brutus as he sat, bowed toward Clitus one of his men, and told him somewhat in his ear: the other answered him not, but fell weeping. Thereupon he proved Dardanus . . . and at length Volumnius, praying him that he would help him to put his hand to his sword, to thrust it in him to kill him. Volumnius denied his request, and so did many others . . . Then Brutus taking every man by the hand, he said these words unto them with a cheerful countenance . . . It rejoiceth my heart, that not one of my friends have failed me; as for me, I think myself happier than those that have overcome, considering that I leave a perpetual fame of our courage and manhood.

Shakespeare arranges the scene so that stage directions for ''alarums'' add a growing note of urgency to Brutus' requests. Octavius and Antony are closing in. We have watched Brutus through a long succession of reverses, in which his noble motives became continually entangled with and frustrated by the realities of the world of political and military action. But the simple statement in Act V, Sc. 5, 34-8 reminds us of the direct, honest, uncomplicated character that he is. He does ''have glory by this losing day'' in a sense in which his opponents can never have it in their victory.

Brutus' dying reference to Caesar indicates again the force that the dead Caesar has exerted throughout the second half of the play. Caesar alive may have been pompous, tyrannical and cruel. Caesar dead, ''the spirit of Caesar'' that Brutus tried to destroy, has been all-powerful. Antony's bloody prophecy, made over his body, has been fulfilled. He was present in the minds (and language) of the conspirators when they quarreled. His ghost, appearing to Brutus, introduced the final movement of the action. Cassius died with Caesar's name on his lips and Brutus, finding Cassius dead, spoke lines which sum up the action of the play: ''O Julius Caesar, thou art mighty yet! /Thy spirit walks abroad and turns our swords/In our own proper entrails.''

In most of Shakespeare's tragedies there comes, at the play's end, a brief, final moment of calm. The conflict of the play has run its course, the hero is dead, and there is usually a speech which concludes the action on a quiet, mournful note. Here the speech is given to Antony, and it is a moving tribute to Brutus' qualities. There is no need to question Antony's consistency here. The passions of the struggle have gone, and Antony and Octavius both speak, not so much as particular characters, but as representative Romans mourning a dead hero without reference to political faction.

68

Structure

Methods of Analyzing Structure

Criteria

The structure of a tragedy is governed by the idea of what constitutes a tragedy. Therefore, the philosophic concepts of tragedy which are briefly discussed here are significant for their *relation to* but not necessarily presence in Shakespeare's tragedy.

The Influence of Greek Tragedy

Aristotle's definition of tragedy stated:

> Tragedy then is an imitation of some action that is important, entire, and of a proper magnitude — by language embellished and rendered pleasurable but by different means in different parts — in the way not of narration but of action — effecting through pity and terror the correction and refinement of such passions.

In this definition, certain terms require explanation: *Imitation* is interpreted not as a mere copy but as a representation of thought or vision. The phrase, "Art imitates nature" is conceived to mean that art creates in the sense that nature creates. *Action* is interpreted to mean experience and the qualities of dramatic action are described as "important," that is, concerned not with commonplace events but with events of extraordinary greatness; "entire," that is, consisting of a beginning, a middle and an end; and "of proper magnitude," meaning that the length must be appropriate to its action, not as a story told but as a story recreated or represented or dramatized. The phrase, "through pity and terror effecting correction" is taken to mean that purgation or purification of the soul which is also known as *catharsis*. The important qualification concerning catharsis is that it takes place when, through participation in the dramatic action, the viewer is released or purged of emotions.

Shakespeare departs from the influence of Greek drama in his non-observance of the classical *unities*. The unities is a concept governing the span of *time, place* and *action* in drama. The unity of time dictates that the action take place within one day; of place, that the action occur within one setting; of action, that there be a single plot of limited involvement. Although Shakespeare was aware of the Greek concept of the unities, he deliberately chose to retain the looser dramatic structure inherited from the medieval European theater.

Scene and Structure

Alfred Harbage considers that the basis of the structure of the Shakespearean play is the scene. The scene is identified as having ended in that interval when, all characters having made exits, individually or separately, the stage is vacant; there is then the entrance of new or other characters, individually or in groups, and when the stage is occupied, a new scene or new action commences. A further characteristic of the scene is that a new scene is conceived of as taking place at a later time and possibly in a different place as well. It is the nature of scenes that they vary in length, in number and in structure according to the nature and not according to the length of the play. Therefore, a short play may have a greater number of scenes than a longer play.

Speech in the Structure of the Scene

In Shakespeare's dramatic structure, speech is the structural unit within the scene. It is apparent that in Shakespeare's plays each speech is first of all a response to another speaker, to an event, to a character's inner need for communication which has been triggered by some action outside the speaker. There are, further, several identifiable forms of speeches characteristic of Shakespeare's plays: *Monologues*, which are speeches of some length purposely addressed to the audience; *Expository speeches*, which are statements covering past or present off-stage action; the *Soliloquy*, in which the speaker is not addressing an audience but is genuinely voicing his thoughts aloud; the *Aside*, a speech, generally short, in which the speaker informs the audience of actions or motives under the convention (or artifical pretence) that the speaker is unheard by the other characters on the stage with him.

The Relation of Setting to Structure

First, in a consideration of place in its relation to the structure of a Shakespearean drama, the scene location in the play reveals the influence of the neutral or unlocalized stage. In other words, place is not indicated unless it is specifically important to the action. This characteristic obviously grew out of the nature of the Elizabethan stage which was unadorned and "unset." However, place was frequently indicated by *hand properties*, which were some portable materials, mention of which was worked into the play or "script" and which fixed the place of the scene for the audience.

Second, in a consideration of the relation of time to the structure of the play, it is evident that time, that is, a particular time of day or night, is indicated only when specifically important, and then through a mention of some natural phenomenon in the script. *Time lengths* between scenes are almost invariably unspecified; time is vaguely "later." The fixed condition concerning time as it affects structure is that time is *chronological in sequence*; in other words, there are no flash-backs in the structure of a Shakespearean play.

A further analysis of "time" in the structure of the play reveals that certain *conventions* or artificialities of time are observed. Among these conventions are *double-time*, a technique, accepted by reader or audience, in which time moves at a different pace for one set of characters or one character than for another. There is also the *telescoping of time*, so that an event which supposedly extends over several hours is represented on the stage in a few minutes.

Questions and Answers on Structure

Question 1.

Since Shakespeare's plays are "traditionally" divided into acts, defend the validity of considering the *scene* as the basic structure of his plays, making all textual references to *Julius Caesar*.

Answer

Students of the drama have traditionally considered that the act is the structural unit of the play, and have considered that each act is constructed with a certain structural purpose as follows: Act I — Introduction; Act II — Complication; Act III — Crisis; Act IV — Resolution; Act V — Outcome. The first objective to such an analysis of the play is that the division of the play into acts was not a part of the original play or acting script, but such division instead constitutes a modern interpretation of the original script. Harbage further points out that in Shakespeare's plays each act is not constructed according to the outline of acts above. With reference to *Julius Caesar*, it cannot be argued that Act I is clearly or only "Introduction" or that Act IV is "Resolution." However, that the scene is the structural basis of the play can be argued from *Julius Caesar*. A consideration of the very first scene of the play, the confrontation of the crowd of plebeians (commoners) by the tribunes reveals that "piece of action" as a clearly established unit of communication, in which time, place, situation, even the "tone" of the impending conflict are conveyed: the time is the moment of arrival of the hero, Julius Caesar, in Rome and it is also a religious commemorative day, the Lupercal; the place is the street, identified as such by the words of the tribunes to the plebeians; the situation of the plebeians' illegal roaming and holiday from their work is condemned by their own representatives, the tribunes, whose guardianship of republicanism requires of the plebeians more faithfulness and intelligence than they are revealing; finally, the "tone" of popular, amiable mindlessness of the crowd as opposed to the strict, somewhat legalistic, but deeply felt, attitudes of the tribunes prefigures the conflict of Brutus with the mob psychology. Another justification for considering the scene as the basis of the dramatic structure may be seen in an analysis of Act III, Scene 2, which, by its length and nature presents itself as a fully conceived "whole" unit, containing "thesis," that is, Brutus' oration to the crowd and "antithesis," Antony's funeral oration and, in the last rush of the mob-audience, the resolution.

Chart: Guide to Main Action and Location

Scene	ACT I	ACT II	ACT III	ACT IV	ACT V
1	(Street in Rome) The tribunes, Flavius and Marullus, disperse the crowds gathered to watch Caesar's triumph. They shame the crowd into leaving and they themselves part to undrape the decorations from Caesar's statues along the street.	(Rome: Brutus' Orchard) Brutus debates with himself about killing Caesar. He reads the letters planted by Cassius. These confirm his decision to join the conspiracy. Conspirators meet with him and decide details, including the time of meeting Caesar to escort him to the Capital. Portia persuades Brutus to share his secret griefs with her. Ligarius is recruited by Brutus to the cause.	(Rome: Before the Capitol) Caesar is escorted to the Forum and petitioned by the conspirators. He denies the petitions and is stabbed. The conspirators spread through the streets to allay people's fears. Antony sends word to Brutus seeking a meeting about Caesar's death. Brutus sends for him; accedes to his request to speak at Caesar's funeral despite Cassius' opposition. Antony, alone with the body, vows vengeance and prophesies a bloody civil war. He sends news of the event to Octavius.	(A House in Rome) The triumvirate (Octavius, Antony and Lepidus) meet and agree on people to be blacklisted. Antony sends Lepidus for Caesar's will which he wishes to alter. He makes plans with Octavius for battle against Brutus' and Cassius' forces.	(The Plains of Philippi) Antony and Octavius discuss the advance of Brutus' and Cassius' forces. A parley with the enemy is called in which both sides insult each other and hurl defiance. Cassius, feeling doom on this, his birth date, takes farewell of Brutus in case this is their last meeting alive.
2	(A Public Place) Caesar orders Antony to touch Calphurnia in the Lupercal games and is warned to beware the Ides of March. Brutus and Cassius discuss Caesar's triumph procession and Casca comes by to give a first-hand account of the offer of a crown to Caesar by Antony. Cassius takes this occasion to broach the subject of Caesar's rising power to Brutus. Brutus agrees to talk with Cassius more about this.	(Caesar's House) Caesar is persuaded by Calphurnia not to go to the Capitol. The conspirators come in and Decius Brutus, as he promised, devises a flattering interpretation to the bad augury, as well as to Calphurnia's urgings, and he persuades Caesar to change his mind. Caesar starts for the Capitol escorted by the conspirators.	(The Forum) Brutus speaks to the crowd in declaration of his deed, reasons and motives, then introduces Antony and leaves. Antony inflames the populace in a clever speech against the conspirators and sets them loose in rage for blood of the plotters. A servant tells him Octavius is already in Rome and with Lepidus, awaits him at Caesar's home. Brutus and Cassius have fled Rome.	(Sardis: Brutus' Tent) Brutus gets word that Cassius wishes to speak to him. He agrees and Cassius starts a complaint. Brutus asks him into the tent to talk privately instead of before the troops.	(The Field of Battle) Brutus sends Messala with orders to the troops to attack because he thinks Octavius' forces are lagging.

Scene	ACT I	ACT II	ACT III	ACT IV	ACT V
3	(A Street) The strange happenings of the night are discussed by Casca and Cicero, and when Cicero leaves, Cassius comes and talks with Casca to enrol him in the conspiracy. Cassius then discusses some details of the conspirators' meeting with Cinna, who asks him to enlist Brutus to the cause. Cassius says to leave it to him; he tells Cinna to throw some letters prepared by Cassius into Brutus' window.	(Street near the Capitol) Artemidorus, a poet, has a letter; he is stationing himself along the way to give it to Caesar; it warns him about the conspirators who are named in the letter.	(A Street) The mob let loose by Antony takes its first victim, Cinna the poet. Even though he is not that Cinna who is a conspirator, he is lynched by the mob in their unreasoning frenzy.	(Brutus' Tent) Brutus and Cassius have a showdown and then they patch up their quarrel. Brutus reveals that Portia is dead (suicide). Messala comes in to report that Octavius and Antony are approaching with a mighty force and that many in Rome of their faction, including Cicero, have been executed. Brutus and Cassius plan their strategy. When Brutus is alone, he is visited by Caesar's ghost which warns him of its coming presence at Philippi.	(Another Part of the Field) Titinius reports Brutus' attack unsuccessful and their forces trapped. Cassius sends Titinius to identify the troops he sees below him and when Pindarus wrongly reports from a hill Titinius dismounted and captured, Cassius runs on his sword with Titinius' help. Titinius kills himself in grief for Cassius. Brutus comes upon the bodies, utters his grief for Cassius and prepares for a last battle.
4		(Street Before Brutus' House) Portia is quite distracted. She sends the boy, Lucius, to Brutus to see how he is, then talks to a soothsayer who voices fears to her for Caesar. She has fears about Brutus' enterprise and cannot trust herself not to give it away. She seems under great emotional strain, near the breaking point.			(Another Part of the Field) Individual combat continues and Brutus runs out shouting defiance. Lucilius is captured and pretends he is Brutus. Antony recognizes who he really is and orders him spared and won over to Antony's camp.
5				ACT V, SCENE V (Another Part of the Field) Brutus' forces are in retreat and Brutus asks each of a number of his followers to help him commit suicide with his own sword. He finally persuades Strato to do so. Octavius and Antony appear victorious on the field, take the various followers of Brutus and Cassius as their own aides and	Antony launches his tribute to Brutus. Octavius orders that Brutus lie in state in his tent and says the final parting words in the play.

Question 2.

What is the relation of the "unities" to *Julius Caesar*?

Answer

As conceived by the Elizabethan playwrights, and as was probably understood by Shakespeare, the "unities" related to unity of time, of place and of action. These unities are not observed in the play, *Julius Caesar*. With relation to time, the "unity" as Elizabethans understood (or misunderstood) the Greek concept was exceeded, although Shakespeare "telescoped" or shortened actual historic time, as in the shortening of the period, for dramatic purposes, between the assassination of Caesar and the victory of the triumvirate and, more clearly in the play, between the quarrel between Brutus and Cassius and the Battle of Philippi. Second, that the unity of place is not observed is obvious from a cursory consideration of "places" in the play: a street, the Capitol, Brutus' orchard, Brutus' tent, the battlefield, and so forth. Finally, the unity of action is ignored in that succeeding scenes introduce whole new sets of characters, the convention of off-stage action reported by a character is resorted to only once (in Casca's report of Caesar's refusal of the crown and swoon at the races) while, in the chronicle-play tradition and not in the Greek tradition, whole battle scenes take place onstage. Therefore, it is clear that the unities of time, place and action as understood in Greek drama are ignored in the play *Julius Caesar*. The unity which makes the play a cohesive whole may be characterized as thematic singleness.

Question 3.

Analyze the nature and the purpose of "the speech" in the play.

Answer

The speech is the structural unit within the scene. To make an analogy, the speech (of a particular kind) is to the scene what the cell (of a particular variety) is to the particular organ of the human body. Each scene, therefore, can be seen as made up of speeches, the variety and number and other characteristics of the speeches dependent on the purpose of the scene which they construct. In *Julius Caesar*, Act I, Scene 2, Cassius speaks at length, claiming "honor" as his theme, relating the physical frailties of Caesar and, in all, making out a serious objection to Caesarism. This speech illustrates a characteristic of the speech: it is first of all a response, in this case, a response to the reaction, lukewarm but favorable, which Cassius has evoked from Brutus and, as communication, it is not an end in itself; it requires a response to it. It is a typical speech in that there is movement in it, a requirement of something further from the speaker himself, from the on-stage character listener, all of which carry the audience, listener or reader, to that something further referred to. An example within that scene of the differentiation of speech as to purpose can be seen from the lines in which Casca reports on Caesar's behavior at the races. This speech is an example of exposition of an action or actions that have gone on elsewhere, yet, typical of the Shakespeare speech, it invites and requires responses such as Cassius' wry play on the meaning of "falling sickness," Brutus' condemnation of Casca and Cassius' very meaningful defense of his quick mettle. Finally, Act I, Scene 2 affords an example of the true soliloquy, in which the character meditates aloud for his own ear or mind. Cassius evaluates the usefulness of Brutus in a possible conspiracy and reveals his own character traits in comparing himself to Brutus. His admission here of the great store he puts on personal affection, that, were he loved by Caesar as Brutus is, he should not conspire against Caesar, is typical soliloquy material, being internal matter, between character and (by the convention of its invisibility) audience.

Question 4.

Identify and discuss the elements which indicate that the structure of the play makes it suitable for presentation on the Elizabethan stage.

Answer

As a playwright whose occupation was writing to provide entertainment for audiences in a theater, Shakespeare constructed *Julius Caesar* with the tastes of his audience in mind. First, the play opens on a jocular note which quickly becomes slashingly serious in the criticizing of the saucy plebeians by the outraged tribunes; the first scene was calculated to hold the noisiest section of the audience through its humor and through its underscored emotionality. The popular taste for violence that lingered in the least cultured segment of the audience, if not elsewhere in the theater-going public, was catered to in such scenes of violence and physical shock as the assassination of Caesar, the lynching of the poet Cinna and the near-hysterical outburst of Cassius in the quarrel with Brutus. The construction of the play so that the element of contrast is basic to it resulted in a secure hold on the interest and understanding by the audience of what it was seeing and hearing on the stage. Some instances of the forms of contrast are in the "tone" of one scene as against the scene that follows it: the violence of the scene in which Antony unleashes the mob after the assassination of Caesar as opposed to the cold, purposeful, quiet planning scene of the triumvirate; in the temperaments of protagonists; in Cassius who is fiery, emotional, highly verbal as opposed to Brutus' laconic, brooding mood in their opening conversation; between philosophies, especially as reactions to unnatural phenomena, that is, manifestations of fear or disregard of danger are shown on the night preceding the Ides of March. Again, historical research indicates that the very choice of Julius Caesar as the subject of a play was in keeping with popular taste for historical narrative, particularly for a chronicle of a hero, historically real or approximately so, larger than life in character, in ambition and in deed. These are only a few of the indications of Shakespeare's remarkable rapport with is audience.

The second consideration of the structure as suitable for the Elizabethan stage involves the techniques of scene building: the unlocalized scene, so suitable for the Elizabethan undressed stage; the "terminal" nature of each scene, whose end is signalled by the exit of its characters; the linguistic structures within the scene to indicate time and place or special properties of the characters as need be. For instance, the "hand properties" or street decorations belonging to Caesar which the tribunes remove, the mention of "grey clouds" signalling the dawn, the identification of time elsewhere through dialogue, the identification of place, as Brutus' tent, through its integral place in the dialogue between him and Cassius.

Characters

Methods of Analyzing Characters

1. Describing the Characters

As a first approach to visualizing a character, one may start with these immediately evident physical and emotional aspects of a character in a drama: *what* is he, *how* does he look or speak? For instance, what can be described about Antony? He is young, an athlete, a special aide to Caesar. This is deduced from his first appearance. He is a runner in the Lupercal games and, called specially by Caesar to touch Calphurnia, he must be of presentable physique and specially favored by Caesar. He must be, most likely, a handsome man — he is "gamesome" according to Brutus, and a reveller. He is well spoken; he ingratiates himself with the conspirators even though, as the special favorite of Caesar, they should have reason to suspect him of hostility. He has stamina: Caesar remarks that Antony, though up nights, is present at an early hour to see him to the Senate.

Sometimes a character eludes one's description because what he does in the play (the purpose he serves for the author) may be more important than what he is, and character analysis and development are unimportant in the same way that a messenger in a play remains only that. He serves the purpose of communication for the author. Casca is not developed as a character, but he serves two purposes: one, to add a "sour" version of Caesar's bid for absolute power and second, to signal the assassination by stabbing Caesar first. Beyond this, he has no importance in the play sufficient for character development.

2. Analysis of Character Development

The best analysis of character comes about through character development skillfully brought about by the dramatist. The main characters, in particular, grow or develop as the play progresses. This development may come about through the *self-appraisal* by the character himself — often in the *soliloquy*. In this very self-appraisal the character may reveal traits he is not talking about or doesn't admit he possesses. For instance, when Caesar talks about his being constant as the northern star and as being the one such shining star among men, he reveals not consistency and constancy but overbearing vanity which reveals his self-image as god-like. Octavius, when he counters Antony's scorn of Lepidus, shows that he possesses an integrity that would not despise a man so beneath him and still use him for his purposes. The development comes through the interaction of the characters upon each other. It is evident in the images and speech of the characters. We have no instance, except what is reported, to show that Caesar would for the sake of flattery alter a pronouncement he has made. It remains for the meeting with Decius Brutus to bring out this trait in Caesar.

3. Motivation

This is a strong force in influencing character and the acts of men and women. Sometimes there is a predominant motivation which throughout a play moves a central character to certain acts and deeds. But it is these acts and deeds, bringing on further complications and reactions from others in the drama, that further motivate and direct the ''springs of human conduct.'' The Macbeth who was early in the play motivated to the crown, is the same Macbeth at the end, but all the facets of his character have been brought out, shaped and directed by the chain of events he let loose with the first murder. We learn that he is a good husband, enjoys having friends and being loved and honored, and has strong regrets for the very deeds he commits. In short, his character developed with the course of events, sparked by a motivation within him and forces without.

To examine why characters do things — their motivation — is one means of beginning character analysis.

4. Reflection or Interaction

One good clue to character analysis lies in the image of the one person as seen by the others in the play, or the reaction to the others by that first character. Even though it is a biased picture, the wry, envious account of Caesar, and the ''sour'' reflections of Casca build the image of Caesar, both his physical nature and his emotional make-up. Caesar's own pronouncements about himself, as well as his acts and decisions, confirm our notions of Caesar's character. That the conspirators want Brutus to head the conspiracy because he will lend honor and dignity and make the cause just, is indicative of much of Brutus' character as well as reputation. If we investigate what others say about a person, some understanding of his character has already been set in motion. Add to this how the person interacts with others, summed up with the self-revelations in the soliloquy, and a character analysis emerges much as the dramatist has planned it in the structure of the play.

Character Sketches

Julius Caesar

The Julius Caesar of history (102 or 100 to 44 B.C.) was a brilliant military and political leader who affected the course of world history.

Shakespeare depicts him at the end of a glorious life, declining mentally and physically, infatuated with himself as a kind of god-like superman. He is deaf in one ear, afflicted with epilepsy, and becoming increasingly dependent on the visions of fortune-tellers. The important character trait in the play is a stubborn belief in his own divinity. This idea stirs resentment and fear in the aristocratic republicans who seek to preserve the republic and their own power, and who therefore conspire to assassinate Caesar before he can make himself king.

Through to Act III, Scene 1, when he is assassinated, Caesar is presented as pompous, vain, arrogant, and increasingly lacking in the ability to understand both the true motives and the behavior of the men around him. It is true that in Act I, Scene 2 he shows keen insight into the character of Cassius ("He is a great observer, and he looks/Quite through the deeds of men.") But elsewhere he fails to recognize the dangers facing him and falls easy prey to the wiles of Decius (Act II, Scene 2), who deftly reinterprets Calphurnia's dream and lures him to his death. Antony's funeral eulogy restores the illusion of Caesar as a dedicated and heroic leader and benefactor of the common people.

The play is entitled *Julius Caesar* because Caesar is the subject and ruling spirit of the play, not its protagonist (leading character). After the assassination, the ghost of Caesar reveals how effectively the spirit of the great leader can still exercise control over the minds of Romans, and even achieve vengeance for his murder.

Brutus

As in all Shakespearean tragedies, the center of the drama is the protagonist, someone with a highly sensitive moral conscience, who suffers and dies because of a tragic weakness in his character or because of a fundamental unsuitability to the role that the world has chosen him to play. Like Hamlet, Brutus is faced with a problem that his best qualities render him unfit to solve. Idealist, stoic, cultured gentleman and scholar, he is wholly unable to understand the everyday complexities of down-to-earth politics and much too high-minded to compromise with the facts of corruption and self-interest that compose the political scene of the Rome of his day. Dedicated to republicanism at a time when it is dissolving from Roman life, he dreams of reviving traditions that cannot be revived and of rallying his contemporaries to a nobility of purpose they cannot themselves understand. His soliloquy at the opening of Act II, Scene 1, in which he tries to convince himself that Caesar must die for the good of Rome, is a masterpiece of characterization, revealing Brutus as an extremely virtuous but deluded man whose head must be forever in the clouds.

Hurled into the political arena, Brutus makes one mistake after another; and Cassius, who knows better, must stand by, helpless against the man's dignity and influence, and make the best of things. First, Brutus refuses to permit a binding oath among the conspirators, insisting instead that they rely on their sense of honor as patriotic gentlemen. The result of this is that one of the conspirators betrays them and soon Artemidorus knows all. Next, he foolishly insists that Antony be permitted to live, completely missing the truth of Antony's shrewd capabilities as politician and military leader. After the assassination, instead of trying to adjust differences with the conniving conspirators, he staunchly persists in forcing them to live up to impractical and idealistic standards of behavior, which they cannot possibly meet. The result is defeat and death.

Cassius enlists the support of Brutus because Brutus is extremely influential and popular enough among the common people to provide the conspiracy with unity and power. But though Brutus is well-intentioned, he cannot perceive the selfishness and hyprocisy of the conspirators and foolishly imagines himself leading them away from tyranny and into a kind of utopian salvation.

But the whole force of the tragedy centers around the basic irony of the man's futility and failure. His best qualities drag him down. Nevertheless, as he struggles for justice and self-understanding, he proves himself an inspiration to other men and also reflects the profound capacity of the human soul for dignity and moral grandeur.

Cassius

Like Brutus in that he is an aristocrat and republican who despises tyranny, Cassius is unlike Brutus in being motivated more by self-interest and envy in plotting against Caesar. Whereas Brutus is reflective, philosophical, idealistic, Cassius is contrastingly quick-witted, practical, and opportunistic. Though cynically aware of Brutus' shortcomings as a political-military leader, Cassius nevertheless determines to use the man's great stature and moral influence to help the conspiracy succeed.

Brutus sees only his idealization of men; Cassius sees them as they are. A shrewd, cynical, realistic manipulator, Cassius plays on their weaknesses to serve himself. In Act I, Scene 2, he flatteringly maneuvers the noble Brutus into joining the conspiracy by working on the man's patriotism and family pride. In Act I, Scene 3, he works on the superstitious Casca with the same success.

Cassius reveals much of himself in the soliloquy at the end of Act I, Scene 2, wherein he reflects cynically on the weakness of Brutus and boasts to himself that had the situation been reversed he would never permit himself to be played upon as he has played upon Brutus. Caesar admires Brutus, but dislikes Cassius, who once served Pompey against Caesar. Thus it is that Cassius has selfish reasons for wanting Caesar out of the way; and he is enough of a politician and psychologist to organize men into getting the job done. But Brutus has the moral grandeur that even Cassius must respect; so Brutus is given command, while the more clever and pragmatic Cassius tries to keep him from bungling details on the way.

Frantic and doubtful before the assassination, Cassius reveals emotional hysteria and threatens to kill himself if the plot fails. Later, in Act IV, Scene III, during the argument with Brutus, he again loses control while Brutus seems tormented by a growing realization that he has compromised his purity of mind for a false goal.

But during the battle scenes that follow, Cassius redeems himself somewhat in courage and in the loyalty he elicits from his followers.

Antony

Shakespeare's Antony is an imposingly handsome, vivacious, deep-feeling man, shrewd at the games of politics and war, passionately loyal to Caesar, but quite capable of making the most of the opportunities provided by his death. The initial impression of him as a harmless playboy wears off after the assassination when Antony connives his way into his enemies' confidence, secures permission to make the crucial funeral address that sways the populace against them, and then sets about to organize and direct the triumvirate that succeeds in defeating the conspirators and their armies on the field of battle.

During the planning of the assassination, Cassius urges Brutus to include Antony along with Caesar, for the shrewd Cassius knows there is much to be feared in this powerful, talented man; but Brutus foolishly argues that Antony will be helpless without his leader. After the assassination, Antony proves Cassius right by delivering so clever and moving an oration that the plebeians are driven to wild acts of vengeance.

Scene 1 of Act IV reveals Antony as an unscrupulous veteran of Roman politics, coldly picking out the names of men who stand in his way, condemning them to death, harshly and mercilessly ridiculing Lepidus, whom he compares to an ass that must be sent grazing once he has outlived his usefulness.

Act V shows Antony as a mature, confident general against whom the younger Octavius must strive to prove himself. The last scene of the play depicts Antony as gracious in victory, a powerful, deeply understanding man, who can give tribute to his enemy in the manner of a truly strong, noble Roman.

Octavius

Octavius is Caesar's nephew and legal heir, about twenty years old, a cool, ambitious, intelligent young man, shown maturing into the someday powerful Emperor Augustus. Deeply loyal to Caesar, Octavius arrives in Rome too late to save him, but hurls himself and his forces into the fight for vengeance with quiet efficiency and growing sense of authority. Scene 1 of Act IV shows Octavius making military and political plans with Antony and replies to him with crisp independence and shrewd judgment. (Antony ridicules Lepidus; Octavius reminds Antony that the man has proved himself a capable soldier.)

In Scene 1 of Act V, Octavius explains Antony's error in having expected the enemy to remain in the "hills and upper regions." When Antony tries to assign the younger man a position in the field of battle, Octavius refuses to accept the older man's judgment in the matter, but asserts himself with remarkable coolness of feeling. In Scene 1 of Act V, before the battle, during the heated exchange of challenges and accusations, Octavius shows an eagerness to avenge Caesar and a brave readiness for combat.

Octavius delivers the final lines of the play, expressing with typical calmness and dignity the authority of a future emperor.

Casca

Shakespeare depicts Casca as a bluff, straightforward, somewhat crusty combat veteran, whose account of Caesar's behavior at the games (Act I, Scene 2) shows impatience with Caesar's pomposity and with Cicero's learned manner. After Casca goes off, Cassius assures Brutus that though Casca affects a "tardy form" (appearance of dull-wittedness), he is actually more intelligent that he seems and can be relied upon in "any bold or noble enterprise." In Scene 3 of Act I, during his conversation with Cicero, Casca reveals a nervous, superstitious temperament in contrast with the controlled intelligence and wisdom of the older, more stable poet. The fact that Casca falls easy prey to the clever Cassius, who quickly misleads him concerning the storm and gets him to commit himself to the conspiracy, reveals that Casca is more hot-headed than he is intelligent. His blow is the first to fall on Caesar; and Antony later (Act V, Scene 1) claims that it was a sly, cowardly blow struck from behind.

Portia

Portia is the wife of Brutus and the daughter of Cato, a well-known Roman patriot and idealist who fought with Pompey against Caesar and finally killed himself rather than suffer ignoble captivity. Portia is depicted as an extremely devoted and courageous wife, equal to the noblest beliefs of her heroic father. In line with stoic belief (the Stoics held that men should be self-controlled and impassively fatalistic concerning the fortunes of their lives), she is determined to share her husband's innermost tensions and to help him face up to them with dignity and courage. She loves Brutus deeply, deliberately gashes her thigh to prove herself equal to his problems, but also shows herself torn between stoic ideals and an uncompromising devotion to her husband's welfare and survival. This conflict explains her suicide, heightens our sympathy for her, and makes her convincingly human as a character and as one of Shakespeare's noblest women.

Calphurnia

Whereas Portia seems a reflection of the noblest part of her husband's nature, Calphurnia is contrastingly weaker in stature and intelligence. It is obvious that she lacks the hold over her husband's mind and feelings that

Portia has over Brutus; and her barrenness, her nervous dreams, her excited addiction to superstition, and her fretful attempt to keep her husband from attending the Senate all seem to make her a weaker, less admirable woman than Portia. Nevertheless, her concern for her husband's safety indicates sincere love, and some of her comments to him in Scene 2 of Act IV show that she is not entirely lacking in spirit and intelligence. ("Alas, my lord!/Your wisdom is consumed in confidence.")

Cicero

Cicero is depicted as a dynamic, outspoken, highly revered orator, a clear-minded spokesman for republican beliefs. In Scene 3 of Act I, the brash, resentful Casca, self-consciously the hardened, down-to-earth soldier, refers contemptuously to Cicero's intellectual superiority; but the line "Those that understood him smiled at one another and shook their heads" implies that Cicero well understood Rome's predicament in the face of Caesar's ambitions and that he would have contributed much to the conspiracy had the conspirators been foresighted enough to include him in their number. Brutus argues that Cicero is too independent-minded to follow where others lead. But it is in the opening dialogue of Scene 3 of Act I that Cicero reveals his character fully. His quiet wisdom in reply to Casca's nervous superstition about the storm shows him as a clear-thinking, philosophical man, too skeptical to accept the nonsense that terrifies the more susceptible Casca.

Ligarius

Ligarius is a sick man whose inspired determination to cast off his kerchief (the linen cloth customarily worn about the head to protect a sick man from drafts) suggests the influence and moral prestige that Brutus has among his fellow Romans.

Publius

Publius is an old Senator who is an innocent and startled witness to the assassination. Cassius sends him home and out of harm's way. (Act III, Scene 1, 85 - 94)

Popilius Lena

Popilius Lena is a Senator who heightens the tension of the assassination scene. As the conspirators prepare themselves, he confronts Cassius and ambiguously wishes him well in his "enterprise," implying that he knows of the plot. When Popilius approaches Caesar to confer with him, Cassius is unnerved into threatening suicide if the plot is discovered. But Brutus notes that Popilius is smiling and that Caesar seems at ease; and Cassius is relieved.

Pindarus

Pindarus is a Parthian captive and attendant to Cassius. In Act V, Scene

3, it is Pindarus whom Cassius sends during the battle to observe how Titinius has been approached by a group of horsemen. Pindarus mistakenly tells Cassius that Titinius has been captured by an enemy troop, when actually the horsemen Pindarus sees are under the command of Messala and are merely greeting Titinius. Discouraged, Cassius then asks Pindarus to stab him. Pindarus obeys, then goes off in despair to leave Rome forever.

Lucius

Lucius is a servant-boy (Act II, Scene 1), whose quiet innocence affects Brutus during trying, reflective moments, and who plays and sings to him soothingly and helps bring out the tenderness and nobility of Brutus' character.

Flavius and Marullus

Flavius and Marullus are tribunes, government officials, actually leaders of the democratic faction or party of the common people, who, despite their own aristocratic background, are sincerely dedicated to the preservation of republican principles of government and therefore strongly opposed to Caesar's growing ambition to make himself king. Both men reveal the high-mindedness and dignity of their class; and their indignation is dramatically effective in laying the groundwork for our understanding of the social-political conflict underway in Rome as the play begins. Marullus predominates, delivering the longest speech of the scene, while Flavius shows a more indulgent tone at the end of the scene.

Lepidus

Lepidus, a wealthy Roman general and member of the triumvirate, whom Antony would send grazing like a retired ass after he has served his purpose, was, as Octavius suggests, a good military leader, but was lacking in the necessary influence to make his political weight felt against the power of Antony. It was Lepidus who, after the assassination, immediately ordered an army into the city to safeguard the interests of the triumvirate.

Decius Brutus

Decius Brutus is the sly, resourceful conspirator who is sent to make sure that Caesar attends the Senate on the fateful day. Decius (whose name is actually *Decimus* Brutus, an error Shakespeare took from Plutarch) flatters Caesar out of his superstitious fear, re-interprets Calphurnia's dream to reassure Caesar into false confidence, and succeeds with subtlety and tact in making Caesar feel that his associates will laugh at him, perhaps think him a coward, if he refuses to attend. In Act III, Scene 1, it is also Decius who steps in between Caesar and Artemidorus in time to prevent the teacher from inducing Caesar to read his petition and learn the truth.

Cinna

Among the conspirators, Cinna is a mere follower, who appears in Scene 3, Act I to be breathlessly involved in conspiratorial preparations; he is also the messenger Cassius sends with papers to be placed in Brutus' chair, urging him to join the plot. In that scene Cinna is glad to learn that Casca has been won into the conspiracy; his enthusiasm suggests the excited mood of the conspirators.

Titinius

Titinius is an officer under Cassius. In Act IV, Scene 3, he is with Cassius at Sardis and is ordered to relay commands to subordinate officers for the encampment of forces and then to return for a military conference. In Act V, Scene 3, as the battle rages, he is at the side of Cassius, sharing his leader's anxieties. It is Titinius who points out that Brutus has erred in giving an attack order too soon. Titinius is unquestioning in obedience ("I will be here again even with a thought."), and when he finds that Cassius has committed suicide, he utters moving words to express his sorrow, his deep loyalty; then he kills himself.

Lucilius

Lucilius is an officer fighting under Brutus and Cassius. His loyalty is so great that he pretends to be Brutus in order to be killed in his place (Act V, Scene 5), but Antony enters, exposes the impersonation, and is so struck with the man's heroism that he determines to take Lucilius into his own service.

Strato

Strato is the loyal servant to whom Brutus turns for the final service of holding the sword while Brutus falls on it. Strato tells Messala that Brutus has achieved glory in death, for he has freed himself from ignoble bondage. Strato's act is considered noble and Octavius is glad to take the man into his own service on the basis of it.

Volumnius

Volumnius is one of Brutus' loyal officers, a school-chum who refuses to hold the sword while Brutus falls on it. ("That's not an office for a friend, my lord.") After the battle, Octavius takes him into his own service, along with Lucilius and Messala, other officers under Cassius and Brutus, on the basis of the loyalty they showed their leaders.

Young Cato

Young Cato is the proud son of the Cato who had fought valiantly for Pompey against Caesar. With great courage, this young officer (Portia's brother) fights to the last (Act V, Scene 4), shouting his challenge to his enemies, even though he knows the cause is lost.

Questions and Answers on the Characters

Question 5.

A close study of any single major character in *Julius Caesar* reveals that the dramatist has "realized" him through a variety of dramatic techniques. Discuss specifically, and in detail, this realization of the character of Antony.

Answer

At the beginning of the play, by Caesar's request that Antony touch Calphurnia against barrenness in the Lupercal games, we infer that Antony is a young, handsome athlete. Next, details about his person and his habits are evident in Brutus' comparison of himself with the character of Antony when Brutus admits he is not "gamesome" nor quick-spirited as Antony is. Later, Caesar remarks that, although Antony stays up late at night enjoying himself, he is, nonetheless, on hand in the morning to escort Caesar to the Capitol. Cassius also sees Antony as a "playboy," though less admiringly. The picture is consistent: Antony is a "playboy" who loves high living, parties, games, etc. Yet, at the same time, there is evidence from his place next to Caesar that he occupies a position of close intimacy with Caesar. For instance, when Caesar says that he fears Cassius, Antony soothes him and is then further sought out by Caesar for his opinion. Such an attitude by Caesar shows that Antony is more than a reveller.

Antony seems bland and ingratiating when he comes seeking the favor of the conspirators. However, quite suddenly he shows his fierce and passionate side when he views Caesar's body. He suddenly possesses a biting tongue which conveys bitterness, sarcasm, defiance. Alone with the body of Caesar, he gives vent to the full rage with which he will later infect the multitude.

And so he does. In the funeral oration yet another facet of his character shines through: he is crafty, subtle, deceitful, histrionic. He is a master of "dirty politics," he is a veritable demagogue in his power to incite the mob.

After this climactic episode in his life, the lighter "gamesome" side of Antony is never again apparent. He has moved to command and he shows arrogance, ruthlessness: he condemns men to death in ruthless fashion; he scorns Lepidus, yet uses him. Finally, all his qualities and powers extended to their full scope, he is matched by Octavius and over him alone he does not hold sway. At the end, in victory, he is able to return to the suave manner of his earlier ways, as he pays tribute to Brutus.

Thus the character of Antony is realized in all its aspects: from a happy, athletic youth to a savage, ruthless political figure. He is present in actions and events in which he reveals himself as bland and then rough and coarse; as a personable, attractive, intelligent confidant to a great man and then as a demagogue, an opportunist and a sophisticated politician. The methods by which this realization of the character of Antony are made involve the reflections of the other characters on him, the weight of his appearances, which increase in frequency and in importance and the decisive role which he plays in so much of the action of the play.

Question 6.

Discuss the meaning of the *tragic flaw* in the Shakespearean hero with references to its occurrence in *Julius Caesar*.

Answer

Possessed of so many virtues and fine qualities, Brutus becomes a figure in tragedy because of the tragic flaw in this fine character. The tragic flaw is not any easily identifiable "bad quality;" on the contrary, one would be hard put to find a malicious or dishonest or reprehensible quality in the man. The tragic flaw in Brutus is that there is a slight, subtle but pervasive undercutting of himself in almost every one of his sterling qualities. For instance, he is an idealist but he is an unrealistic idealist. Therefore his idealism, put to the test, is no match for ruthlessness, cynicism and deceit. Brutus has a conscience — but it hampers him as a guilty conscience. He goes into a cause, an action, against all his unflawed reasoning. He lets himself be flattered into joining the conspiracy, urged on by a concept of ancestral honor. He spends endless days and nights convincing himself against his better nature, for his theory of Julius Caesar, so to speak, is at war with his personal experience of Caesar. His devotion to the abstract virtues, which indeed are what he lives by, remove him from the common arena in which most men live and he is consequently so poor a judge of men's character as to prepare the ground for his own disaster. Firmly decisive on the point that none but Caesar shall die, the "flaw" in Brutus will not let him compromise his principles to the extent of protecting the action, the assassination, already taken. In his refusal to arrange the elimination of Antony lay the seed of his disaster and the downfall of his cause. Finally, his own conscience saw the killing of Caesar as murder, necessary, even glorious in terms of the state, but murder, nonetheless and, his own conscience decided that, although the cause for which he struck was a noble one, the price had to be paid, even if the price be himself. It is his guilty conscience which lets down the barrier through which the spirit of Caesar enters his subconscious and then his conscious being to bring about his defeat. In other words, the nature of Brutus is such that it contains in every virtue a subtle consequence of harm to him and this is the tragic flaw which through his actions, his interactions, his emotions and his intellectual processes brings him to his end; yet, his death itself is not the tragedy. The tragic flaw has brought about the *waste* of all the virtues, the love and the life-values of the man, Brutus.

Question 7.

Why is this play called *Julius Caesar*, when Caesar dies in the third act and Brutus has such a consistent place in the drama from the first act to the fifth?

Answer

Many critics have debated the question of who is the chief protagonist of the play. While the play is preeminently the tragedy of Brutus and even of Cassius, Shakespeare meant it also to be the tragedy of Caesar because Caesar, or his spirit, dominates the lives of all the characters right to their tragic end and even to the happy end that Antony and Octavius reap.

Brutus is haunted by the threat of Caesarism, a projection of Caesar, to the body politic before the assassination, and he is haunted by Caesar's spirit to his mortal end, when he says:

Caesar, now be still.
I killed not thee with half so good a will.

Cassius is bitter, contemptuous and envious of the living Caesar because of his continued dominance and because of his potential further claims to power. Yet after the assassination, so greatly wished, so strongly engineered by Cassius, although not beset by an inner troubled spirit as Brutus, he too succumbs to the dominant spirit of Caesar:

Caesar, thou art revenged
Even with the sword that killed thee.

Certainly in Elizabethan times the legendary Caesar dominated people's thoughts as a figure of imposing greatness. There were a number of plays about Caesar and many books, some in translation, appeared on the power and rule of princes. Certainly Elizabeth's rule had the aspects of a Caesar's in the unlimited power and the beginnings of dominance on the seas. Further, in Elizabethan times, the figure of Caesar as seen in this play would be realized as that of a tragic hero: a great "prince," a focus of power, the single figure who represented the might and glory of the state to the populace, a Caesar could not be killed without grave and harmful consequence to the body of the state. Therefore, it is not surprising that in this play, where the chief character is killed in the third act, he and his spirit should prevail and should take final retribution from the others.

Question 8.

Cassius is a foil for Brutus, for Cassius is the hardcore realist and Brutus the unrealistic idealist and intellectual. Show how they come to accept each other's way of life, and how their opposing natures eventually synthesize.

Answer

One can see a parallel, limited in the extent to which the pairs' of personalities differ, in Brutus' and Cassius' relationship with that of Don Quixote and Sancho Panza. One instance will define the parallel: Don

Quixote, his imagination inflamed with the chivalric code of righting wrong, hurls his defiance and himself upon the windmills, thinking them to be the enemy dragon from whom he must rescue the honor of womanhood and the courage of manhood. In spite of Sancho's pleading with him that these are but wooden blades of a windmill, he rushes on full tilt while Sancho covers his eyes from the rude shock his master will get. Thus, when Brutus says he puts honor and trust above all else and declares this to be his code of living, Cassius tells him that honor is the subject of his story and he goes on to make a bitter comment against Caesar. If Brutus is going to charge head-on against anything, in the name of honor, let it not be a harmless windmill, an abstract quality, honor *per se*; Cassius offers him a real, tangible target. He brings Brutus to the reality of Rome and out of the clouds of abstract virtue. The realistic Cassius has further opportunities for looking away in dismay as Brutus charges head-on with unrealistic decisions at the last meeting of the conspirators to work out the details of the assassination. For instance, Brutus dismisses Cicero, suggested by Cassius as a candidate for the conspiracy. Later events, the fact that Cicero is among the first put to death in the proscription lists of the triumvirate, indicate his merit as a candidate for the forces opposing Caesar. Brutus is against the elimination of Antony even though Cassius repeatedly warns him against him. It is Antony who sparks the turning of the populace on the conspirators. It remains finally for the confrontation at the beginning of their campaign against the forces pursuing them (Octavius' and Antony's) to remove their counter play. In the parley Brutus again overrides Cassius' plan, which, again, results show to have been the more realistic. Yet, after they have had their quarrel and reaffirmed friendship, their actions synthesize. Cassius takes on some of the melancholia of guilt and the sense of impending death which Brutus has carried with him since the assassination and when they part, they are increasingly alike in temperament and in feeling. Cassius, formerly so epicurean in his life-attitudes, has taken on some of Brutus' stoic endurance while Brutus, albeit of iron reserve, has in the quarrel with Cassius showed himself capable of emotionality and testiness. They are more significantly alike in that each regards the other as the man most true, most worthwhile in his life; Cassius, dying, laments that he lives so long as to see his best friend captured, and Brutus, ready to die, is satisfied at least that Cassius (among others) has not betrayed him. Finally, as each dies, the retribution of Caesar upon him is similar, for Caesar's justified vengeance is the last concern of each. Thus, the hard-core realist and the idealist, though initially apart, have synthesized in their philosophy of life and in the searching examination of their own guilt.

Meaning

Methods of Analyzing Meaning

1. The Nature of Meaning

The writer of a piece of fiction gives meaning to his work in many ways, and those ways depend in great part on the type of fiction he has chosen to use as his medium. A dramatist, then, gives meaning to his work in ways that differ from those of a novelist. The reader of a piece of fiction also gives meaning to the work he is reading according to the requirements of the medium: the reader, if he is experienced and sophisticated, knows that he should give different meaning to the novel he is reading from the meaning he assigns to the play he is reading. In other words, the form of the work is an integral part of the meaning. Consequently the drama will have yet further ranges of meaning: for the players who enact it on the stage and for the audience who takes in the drama through eyes and ears, through perception and imagination. The last three named ways of apprehending meaning apply both to the reader and to the audience of the dramatized play.

2. Plot as a Key to Meaning

As the first question one asks about a literary work in identifying it on any plane is likely to be ''What is it about?'' it is apparent that the plot is a key or a handle by which to grasp the meaning. It must be emphasized that plot and meaning are not synonymous: the plot is the *scheme* or the *plan* or the *structure* of a literary work. As such it may contain or exemplify the meaning.

3. Stating the Theme

When the scheme, the plot, is known, the reader is in a position to consider the thought behind the plot which unifies it: the theme. The theme is itself a subject; it is the base from which the structure of the play may have been conceived, as in a piece of music it is the base on which composition and variation depend. A play has meaning in terms of its theme. Some *central idea* pervades a drama: ambition, jealousy, indecision. The fact that there may be more than one concept involved in the theme of a play reminds one of the ''nature of meaning'' already touched on, and the variety of meanings arrived at under a variety of circumstances. The student must, through a knowledge of the plot and through an understanding and recognition of the central idea, reach the theme. He may find full or partial statements of the theme in the words of characters as well as in the action or events.

4. Meaning and Character

The actions of the characters and their voiced opinions may help to determine meaning for the reader. Likewise, a character may be used as the "mouthpiece" for the playwright, voicing (believably or not) the set, personal opinion of the playwright. For instance, Hamlet's advice to the players is generally considered to be Shakespeare's wishes for actors in his own time and place.

5. How to Substantiate Meaning

Assuming that the reader has formulated to his own satisfaction a statement of the meaning of a drama he has read and studied, he may, as a student, have next the responsibility of justification and substantiation of his statement of meaning. He will need then methods of marshalling all the evidence he can develop beyond the evidence offered by the plot, by textual reference to theme and by evidence of actions and words of characters. He will check his understanding of the meaning against the evidence offered by these three major sources first; he will then determine further indications of meaning from a consideration of *significance of the setting*: does the dramatist's selection of time and place lend itself to the overall meaning? For instance, does the upper-bourgeois conventionality evident in the time and place which constitute the setting of Ibsen's *A Doll's House* fall in with an understanding of the meaning of the play as a protest against prisons, for instance the "prison" of the marriage of an upper-class, conventionally idle woman. The reader will find further clues to meaning in the *language* in which the work is written. For instance, if a theme in *Pygmalion* by G. B. Shaw is that language reveals the man, then the flowing, Welsh-derived and hypnotic rhetoric of Alfred Doolittle, the dustman, is valuable evidence of the meaning.

6. Beyond the Central Meaning

After the central theme has been established, the reader and student will be able to establish theories as to the theme or subordinate thematic materials. For instance, if one establishes "vaulting ambition" as a key to the central meaning of *Macbeth*, there is apparent the secondary thematic material concerned with parenthood or the establishment of lineage and this theme adheres to the central meaning through the reasons for ambition, the nature of Macbeth's marriage and the nature of his crimes against Macduff as well as the reasons for his crime against Duncan.

Questions and Answers on Meaning

Question 9.

Describe the basic meaning of *Julius Caesar*.

Answer

Like any interpretation, the attempt to fix the meaning of this play cannot be definitive. Many critics have written on this and as many have differed on the meaning. For instance, eminent British critics maintain that the security of the state, the tragedy of those who would misguidedly alter the necessary course of history, is central, while eminent American critics (Kittredge, for one) argue that the death of liberty, through the failure of Brutus and his colleagues, is the central meaning. But while one's view of the basic meaning may depend on one's philosophical outlook, there is, nevertheless, agreement that there is a central meaning of *honor* in *Julius Caesar*. Brutus stakes his all on it, Cassius has something to say about it, Antony speaks of Brutus (sarcastically or not) as the "*noble* Brutus." As in his tribute at the end, "This was the *noblest* Roman of them all," the word "noblest" has the connotation of honesty and integrity. Brutus' own first statement of his intention flatly declares "I love/The name of honor more than I fear death."

He maintains to Antony after the assassination that the reasons of the conspirators have been full of "good regard," that is, full of good intentions and honorable purposes. Brutus will have the conspirators bind themselves by honor only. Cassius, considering how to attract Brutus into taking action against Caesar, decides that although Brutus is honorable, his "honorable metal" may be "wrought" or persuaded, for there is no one so firm that he cannot be "seduced." And, because Brutus is led to take part in the assassination and because he and Cassius see their own deaths as retributive for this deed, we may infer that the meaning of honesty is indeed couched in Cassius' view: no man is composed purely of honesty and integrity.

Question 10.

Examine the twin themes of Caesarism and Republicanism with reference to their existence in *Julius Caesar*.

Answer

The plot for the assassination has apparently been formed against tyranny. Cassius starts the train of thought:

There was a Brutus once that would have brooked
Th' eternal devil to keep his state in Rome
As easily as a king.

Brutus then indirectly assents to the implied suggestion here:

Brutus had rather be a villager
Than to repute himself a son of Rome
Under these hard conditions as this time
Is like to lay upon us.

Cassius, speaking of his readiness to kill himself, says that by suicide he will shake off "tyranny." The cry after the assassination is "Liberty!

Freedom! Tyranny is dead!'' Cassius sees the conspirators enshrined through the ages:

> So oft as that shall be,
> So often shall the knot of us be called
> The men that gave their country liberty.

In Brutus' speech after the assassination the freedom issue is again raised:

> Had you rather Caesar were living,
> And die all slaves, than that Caesar were
> Dead, to live all freemen?

> Who is here so base that would be a bondman?

We shall return to the question of this theme as it fades in the aftermath of Antony's speech. Let us now examine the meaning of Caesarism.

The first to sound the note of dissatisfaction with Caesarism was the tribune Flavius:

> These growing feathers plucked from Caesar's wing
> Will make him fly an ordinary pitch,
> Who else would soar above the view of men
> And keep us all in servile fearfulness.

Antony is the next one to give us a view of Caesarism as a thing that exists:

> When Caesar says 'Do this,' it is performed.

Cassius' whole bitter complaint is about Caesarism. One of his less sarcastic statements of it would indicate that one-man, absolute rule is what is meant here:

> When went there by an age, since the great flood,
> But it was famed with more than one man?

He further defines it in persuading Casca to the cause:

> Now could I, Casca, name to thee a man
> Most like this dreadful night,
> That thunders, lightens, opens graves, and roars
> As doth the lion in the Capitol;
> A man no mightier than thyself or me

In personal action, yet prodigious grown
And fearful, as these strange eruptions are.

Brutus has nothing to say against Caesar personally, but one possibility
he takes exception to:

Crown him that,
And then I grant we put a sting in him
That at his will he may do danger with.

It would seem that the "kingship" poses the biggest threat of
Caesarism. Previously Casca and Cassius had predicted this threat:

Casca: Indeed they say the senators tomorrow
Mean to establish Caesar as a king,
And he shall wear his crown by sea and land
In every place save here in Italy.
Cassius: I know where I will wear this dagger then;
Cassius from bondage will deliver Cassius.

The meaning seems to be that this kingship would hand over to Caesar
absolute power, though its not having validity in Italy may mean that he gets
equal absolute power over the empire as he has as a Caesar in Rome. Yet
Brutus thought Caesar dangerous not before, but only should he get the
crown. It is Caesarism that is being struck at. Brutus puts it as the discrimina-
tion that he would like to make:

O, that we could come by Caesar's spirit,
And not dismember Caesar!

Caesar himself never questions his own authority but frequently speaks
of his invulnerability:

danger knows full well
That Caesar is more dangerous than he.

It is only once or twice that he shows in himself that he is absolute.

The cause is in my will: I will not come.
That is enough to satisfy the Senate; . . .

Know, Caesar doth not wrong, nor without cause
Will he be satisfied.

Yet in the number I do know but one

That unassailable holds on his rank,
Unshaked of motion, and that I am he, . . .

Here is the issue of Caesarism and the cry opposed to it, as Cassius urges the conspirators at the assassination:

and cry out
'Liberty, freedom and enfranchisement!'

The last word on deliverance from bondage comes from Brutus, as quoted above from his speech defending the assassination of Caesar. The people themselves, running with the tide, just as they had been accused of by the tribunes at the beginning, seem to make no fine distinctions between freedom and bondage. When Brutus had explained in such direct and forth-right terms why he had killed Caesar, the cry was "Let him be Caesar."

It would seem that the meaning of the play is that Caesarism is a threat to the freedom of men and the conspirators have acted as liberators of Rome. The distinction of added power and danger through kingship as opposed to Caesarism remains unexplained and the meaning left to the reader's interpretation or to research into the history of the government of Rome and the Roman empire.

Shakespeare wrote at a time when Elizabeth ruled as a determined monarch subjecting Parliament to her will, aided by Star Chamber proceedings, which hunted treason and tracked it down ruthlessly. It is unlikely that Shakespeare, even if he were not a loyal subject, would be so rash as to write a play against monarchy or kingship; the monarch herself patronized the Players' company. Nor did Shakespeare write plays as tracts against either government or any one of the evil practices of man.

Furthermore, we return now to the question of tyranny and the re-publicanism for which the assassination struck a blow. This idea disappears after the assassination. When Brutus and Cassius confront Antony and Octavius, they quarrel with them peevishly, but neither says anything about having struck a righteous blow for freedom. They make no attempt to talk over the other to their thinking. Instead, the whole conflict becomes a personal one with Brutus and Cassius, both aware of oncoming death; and when they die, both give credit for their deaths to the vengeance of Caesar's spirit. There is no declaration by either as they die that they have set the cause of freedom in motion and could be satisfied for the cause. Brutus declares some vague generalization on this issue:

I shall have glory by this losing day
More than Octavius and Mark Antony
By this vile conquest shall attain unto.

Thus, the meaning of Caesarism versus republicanism is never resolved for us, but the existence of the two has been defined in the play.

Question 11.

To what extent is the action and the nature of the Roman populace central to the meaning of *Julius Caesar*?

Answer

Although the central meaning of the play is bound up with the concept of honor as a guiding precept for action in life, the nature and action of the crowd is a counterpoint to that central meaning. The first image presented in Act I, Scene 1, is of the fickle, amusement-seeking, forgetful crowd of plebeians, who need to be reminded by their very protectors, Flavius and Marullus, how unfairly short-lived their affections are. These tribunes, calling them "worse than senseless things," imply that the crowd is not a human entity, but something less than human, something not made up of the recognizably human qualities of faith and remembrance. Much less than human, then, is the crowd who cheered Brutus' explanation of the killing of Caesar, and then, moved emotionally rather than intellectually, cheered and wept with Antony as he lashed out against the assassins. When he loosed the crowd, they were clearly "worse than senseless things," for without sense, without meaning, they ripped apart the poet Cinna in, sheer sub-human blood-lust. Therefore, it becomes inescapably apparent in this play that the crowd, the mob, is less than the least single human individual; the crowd is fickle, undependable and senselessly murderous.

Question 12.

Explain the use of supernatural elements as an Elizabethan stage convention with reference to *Julius Caesar*.

Answer

Unnatural phenomena relating to weather, such as quakes, storms or fire, were recognized as omens that unnatural events would occur in the world of men. That these events would not concern the humble person but rather the great ones of earth was expressed by Calphurnia. To Elizabethans, to whom the explanations of physical science were mysterious, events pertaining to weather and climate still retained some of the magical. Shakespeare drew on this traditional concept, not only in the storm before the Ides of March, but also in the matter of the birds which followed Cassius to Philippi: first his forces were accompanied by birds of good omen, then these fled and carrion birds, the worst possible omen, flew with them. The birds of ill-omen, appearing when they did, telegraphed a message to Shakespeare's audience, familiar with the convention of meaning conveyed through birds. Most significant is the appearance of the ghost of Caesar, for, in the mind of an Elizabethan, the appearance of a ghost signified guilt (though not necessarily that of the viewer of the ghost) of a wrong that must be righted. The appearance of a ghost forewarned that a wrong would be righted and, consequently, the appearance of the ghost of Julius Caesar foretold misfortune only to those who had caused his death. Therefore, the elements of the supernatural, in terms recognizable to the Elizabethans through their beliefs and their traditions, gave additional moral meaning to the play.

Style

Methods of Analyzing Style

"Style" is the writer's unique way of using his language, not only to convey his full intellectual meaning, but also to create that emotional climate which is equally a component of his work.

Method of Study

Style begins with an author's words, his diction; that is, his habitual choice of words, or his vocabulary, is a component of his style and so is his manipulation of them. This study will begin with a consideration of the author's manipulation of *words* for auditory effect and for intellectual or emotional content.

Qualification for Shakespeare

In any consideration of Shakespeare's dramatic technique, including style, it is necessary to bear in mind that the *words*, the *lines*, the whole of the *play-script* were intended by the author for the ear, to be heard rather than to be read. The play-script itself is just part of a complex art form: the acted drama. Therefore, meaningful analysis requires that passages be read aloud and that the ear must be receptive to meanings not necessarily apparent to the eye.

Diction

Since the first consideration here is the relation of style to the hearing of the play, the first analysis of words is in terms of their sound. *Onomatopoeia* is a rhetorical or literary device involving the use of words whose sound suggests the sense. For instance, the scolding of the plebeians by the tribune (Act I, Scene 1), "You blocks, you stones, you worse than senseless things," suggests actual blows by the blunt, strong monosyllables, and the repeated "s" suggests the hiss of a whip. In this way, selection of words suggests and reinforces the harshness of the tribune's scolding. The device of *alliteration* (the arrangement and selection of words so that there is the repetition of an initial consonant) creates an effect through the ear. Consider how, in Calphurnia's description of disturbed nature (Act II, Scene 2) —
"And graves have yawn'd and yielded up their dead," — the repetition of the "y" sound adds to the eeriness of the statement. In the lines following:

Fierce fiery warriors fought upon the clouds
In ranks and squadrons and right form of war

the alliterative "f's" in the first line and "r's" in the second line, by their hard, sharp sounds, emphasize the martial or warlike meaning of the image. *Punning*, the play on words that have identity or similarity in sound but not in meaning is native to Shakespeare. For instance, in Act I, Scene 1, the cobbler's puns — awl-all, soul-sole — are examples of the *pun for the sake of humor*, since these puns establish the ready wit and impertinence of the cobbler. However, *puns are used throughout the plays for intensification of meaning or mood*. For example, when Antony says of Caesar, "Here wast thou bayed, brave hart," the ear and the mind sort out hart-deer and heart-dear and, in the hearer's emotion, both concepts, the noble, hunted creature and the beloved one, overlay each other so as to emphasize the mournful love which Antony conveys.

Stylistic Devices

One of the rhetorical devices by which the meanings of words are sharpened and expanded is in Shakespeare's use of the *double epithet*. This is the linking (by *and*) of two nouns, verbs, or modifiers of exactly or nearly exactly the same meanings. Several examples from *Julius Caesar* are given below:

Our *yoke and suffrance* show us womanish
. . . .
Our *youth and wildness* shall no white appear
. . . .
Which by the *right and virtue* of my place
. . . .
O *insupportable and touching* loss

The juxtaposed epithets extend with precision and conciseness the meaning and the tone of the line, as in "youth and wildness." In the association there is often a clue to the Latinate word; note that many a word of Anglo-Saxon origin is linked with a word derived from the Latin: "insupportable" (Latin) explained by "touching," and "suffrance" by "yoke."

Another rhetorical device is known as *apostrophe*: the speaker turns away from his audience to make an abstract comment. When Cassius says, "O ye gods, ye gods! must I endure all this?" he is not responding to Brutus' angry words but, instead, turns away from him and addresses the gods. The device intensifies the emotional tone and makes it more evident that Cassius is near the breaking point. Another example of this device is found in Titinius' last words: "Come, Cassius' sword, and find Titinius' heart."

Hyperbole (artistic, deliberate *overstatement*) is used to heighten an effect, as in Brutus' lament over Cassius' dead body: "The last of all the Romans, fare thee well." Cassius is, of course, not the last, but to Brutus he seems to be the last of a kind of Roman. In so describing him, the forlorn and grieving feelings of the survivor are conveyed.

Imagery

The suggestive power of words is exercised through the creation of images which are, in the broad sense, ideas or concepts or such *mental representations as stimulate the senses*. An image represents the poet's imagination reaching out to the reader's (or audience's) imagination. Since there are more varieties of imagery than can be treated here, the following discussion is only a sampling of some of the types of imagery Shakespeare created in his plays. *Metaphors* are, technically, comparisons of two unlike things in which the comparison word "like" or "as" is omitted; a metaphor requires interpretation because the *significant* similarity must be identified among the more obvious dissimilarities. (Formal classification of various forms of metaphoric language as personification, synecdoche, periphrasis, etc. will not be made here.) The discussion below concerns the *effect* of the metaphor.

Brutus, in a single reflective speech about Caesar, resorts twice to metaphoric language. The first instance occurs when he remarks, "It is the bright day that brings forth the adder." This succinct, maxim-like statement reveals, by its choice of the adder as comparable to the Caesar of the future, the emotional revulsion Brutus feels; the almost riddling statement gives with exactness the full set of circumstances that Brutus fearfully envisions. So, the metaphor gives *emotional tone* and suggests *full details*. Second, still talking about Caesar, Brutus says, "Lowliness is young ambition's ladder," and so metaphorically telegraphs to the listener or reader his unspoken fears of what Caesar will do.

A series of *related* figures of speech known as *extended imagery* occur in the drama. When Cassius asks, "Upon what meat does this our Caesar feed?" the word "meat" is meant to suggest "source of power;" Caesar, however, looks at Cassius and thinks of food in its own right, seeing Cassius as "lean and hungry" and therefore dangerous. Brutus thinks of the coming assassination of Caesar as a sort of ritual slaughter: "Let us carve him as a dish fit for the gods." But Antony, looking upon the dead Caesar, sees him as "thou bleeding piece of earth" and speaks of the assassins as "butchers." In all of these cases the metaphor heightens and directs the *emotional tone* through the exercise of the listener's or reader's imagination and experience.

Ambiguity

The quality of *ambiguity* in literature refers to presentation in a veiled or *indirect manner* so that *more than one meaning or effect* may be experienced from it. Ambiguity is a characteristic of much of the imagery, as the example and explanation which follow should indicate:

> O setting sun,
> As in thy red rays thou dost sink to night,
> So in his red blood Cassius' day is set!
> The sun of Rome is set. Our day is gone;

In these lines (Act V, Scene 3), Titinius' words, the phrase "Our day is gone" *has three-fold meaning*: the passing of the physical day; the end of Cassius' "day" or time on earth; and the passing of an era.

The Media

Shakespeare wrote *Julius Caesar* in three media: prose, rhyming couplets and blank verse. Although *blank verse* is by far the most important and most typical, the qualities of the other two media should also be noted.

Prose: The first quality noted in the prose is its *rhythm*, a musical pattern, but not regular as the meter of the verse. The second quality of the prose is its *richness in imagery*. The functions of the prose in *Julius Caesar* are several. It is used to present the prosaic or the commonplace. For example, when Brutus, Cassius, and the "blunt Casca" discuss Caesar's actions at the races, they speak in prose. Not only the diction but the rhythm of their speech maintains report-like, unemotional tone. Prose is also used to emphasize the deliberately rational, especially in contrast to the highly emotional. The tone of Antony's oration is highly charged with emotion; it is in blank verse. Again, prose is used where it would appear noticeably unnatural to use verse: it is used in *letters*, as, for instance, the letters Brutus received, supposedly from liberty-loving Romans. Finally, prose is used in introductory or transitional scenes.

Rhymed Verse: A small proportion of *Julius Caesar* is rhymed, chiefly in the form of *capping couplets* like the following:

And after this let Caesar seat him sure
For we will shake him or worse days endure.

Capping couplets appear at the end of a scene or at the end of a speech; they consist of one or more pairs of rhyming couplets. Their purpose is to give a speech or scene a concluding flourish.

Blank Verse: The most important of all the media is the blank verse. Shakespeare's command of blank verse is supreme in the English language. There are several major characteristics of Shakespeare's blank verse. The line is *decasyllabic*, containing *ten* syllables or, frequently, an *unaccented eleventh syllable* called a *feminine ending*. When there is a *natural stopping place* at the end of a line, the line is called *end-stopped*. When the *meaning* of one line *carries over* to the next, it is called a *run-on line* or *enjambment*. The effect of these modifications on the basic decasyllabic line is to carry the thought with great flexibility and to reduce, but not obliterate, the basic measure.

The basic measure of blank verse is the division of the ten-syllable line into five feet of two syllables each. Each metrical "foot" is called an *iamb*; since there are five iambs in a line of Shakespeare's blank verse, a line is known as *iambic pentameter*. To *scan* a line is to mark off the measured stress or *meter* with a symbol for each accented syllable ($\acute{x}$) and for each unaccented syllable (x̆). When there is a difference between the beat of the measured stress and the emphasis required by the meaning of the line (called *significant stress*) the reader may vary from the measured stress according to the best judgment of his intellect and ear. Below are illustrations of the craft of verse in *Julius Caesar*:

1. Ŏ míght y̆ Cáe săr! dóst thŏu líe sŏ lów?
   a) This is an example of a line of iambic pentameter without variation.
   b) The line is end-stopped.

2. The torrent roared, and we did buffet it
   With lusty sinews, throwing it aside
   And stemming it with hearts of controversy;
   a) The first two lines are run-on, or examples of enjambment.
   b) The third line has an eleventh (weak) syllable or feminine ending.

Questions and Answers on Style

Question 13.
Analyze specific examples of language in *Julius Caesar* with reference to the effects created.

Answer
There is in the play a frequent employment of *axiomatic brevity*, as in the words spoken by Calphurnia to Caesar (Act II, Scene 2) in warning against his intention of proceeding to the Capitol:

"Your wisdom is consumed in confidence."

The statement is, of course, axiomatic or self-evident; that an excess of self-confidence suggests a foolish lack of care is a recognizable human experience. The brevity with which this wise saying is expressed gives it an intensity and urgency which rightly express the "tone" of Calphurnia's warning and mood, particularly in view of her sensed rather than spoken fears. Although Caroline Spurgeon finds in *Julius Caesar* somewhat fewer images than in other tragedies, certain vivid images in the play convey meanings of several varieties and on several levels. Notice, for example, the words of Cassius to Brutus concerning Caesar's position in the world (Act I, Scene 2):

Why, man, he doth bestride the narrow world
Like a Colossus, and we petty men
Walk under his huge legs and peep about
To find ourselves dishonorable graves.

Comparison in these lines is stark, vivid, dramatic, and even jolting to the mind and senses, as it is meant to be. In the first line, Caesar is placed in reference to the world: he is so mighty, of such consequence, that he "bestrides" the world; the world is characterized as "narrow" because he is so mighty in it. In the first line, also, the stance of Caesar, who "bestrides" the world is a vivid image before the eyes and this is stressed further with a related image, that of the Colossus. Then comes the second comparison, of other men in relation to Caesar; other men are "petty;" they are so small as to "walk about under his huge legs," not even shoulder high to the superman, Caesar. Being so tiny, their vision is described with a minimizing verb: they do not scan horizons or search the skies, but "peep about" only to find "dishonorable graves," there being, of course, nothing else for them. Thus, in four lines, through a series of images and contrasts, Shakespeare has created in the reader's mind and perceptions Cassius' state of mind: dissatisfaction and disgust. A third linguistic construction is found in figurative language, as in Act IV, Scene 3:

> There is a tide in the affairs of men
> Which, taken at the flood, leads on to fortune;
> Omitted, all the voyage of their life
> Is bound in shallows and in miseries.

Here the figure is of man the voyager, the sea voyager, who must set sail with the tide or else waste away in shallow waters forever after. The meaning, that man must seize opportunity when it presents itself or be content to live in failure ever after, is apparent to the intellect, of course, but the figures of the mariner and the sea voyage give emotional and aesthetic overtones of distance, of the mystery and finality of tides, of the weed-grown shallow waters, lending depth to the meaning, to the feelings of the speaker (Brutus), and giving the words the seriousness of a prophetic pronouncement.

Question 14.

What is *iterative imagery* and how is it apparent in *Julius Caesar*?

Answer

The theory of iterative imagery involves the interpretation of a drama in terms of the recurrent words or images in a given category. For instance, there is throughout the play *King Lear* a recurring reference to clothing and nakedness; some scholars have developed the theory of "divestiture" — that is, that the imagery tends to develop to a final nakedness, signifying purity. The meaning of *Macbeth* may be studied in terms of the images of birds, the image of blood and blood-letting and the image of dark, or dark and evil. These are recurrent and progressive images. In a study observing the technique of iterative imagery, the student has the responsibility of scrupulously retaining the meaning of the image within the framework of the play. Now although in *Julius Caesar* there is less imagery than in the tragedies touched on above, a study of the iterative image could be made in terms of the comparisons of characters to animals: Cassius is compared by Brutus to a spirited but undependable horse; Lepidus is compared by Antony to an old, faithful plug of a horse. All but one comparison of man to beast is unfavorable to the man. (The possible exception is Brutus' comparison of himself to a lamb). In the instances mentioned the image has relevance to a particular action within the play as well as applicability to the whole structure of the tragedy.

Question 15.

Discuss a specific example of a problem of connotation of the language in *Julius Caesar*.

Answer

In contrast to denotation, which is the actual or literal meaning of a word, connotation includes that which the word suggests or implies in addition to its actual meaning. For instance, to an American suburbanite, the expression, "My husband enjoys relaxing in his den," probably conveys an image of a man comfortable with book or newspaper or hobby materials in a casually furnished room. On the other hand, it is quite possible that the same statement would evoke startled astonishment in a Scotsman, who conceives of a den as a wild animal's lair. In this case, environment is the deciding factor in the connotation of the term. In *Julius Caesar*, the word which is most interesting in the significance of its connotation is *ambitious*. When Brutus says that Caesar was killed because he was ambitious, the meaning which registered in the minds of the Elizabethan audience was of a word considerably more unfavorable than the word ambitious is in twentieth century United States or England. To the Elizabethan, and as Shakespeare intended, the word ambitious signified that which is *unlawfully* desirous or pretentious; in the sense that Caesar was desirous of supreme and sole rule and power, he was *ambitious*. Therefore, when Brutus called him ambitious he was criticizing, not merely characterizing, Caesar. The historical connotation of this word is required knowledge, then, for the discerning modern reader.

*Unity in Julius Caesar

Modern readers are prone to find the tragedy of Brutus in his rigid devotion to justice and fair play. Many members of the Globe audience, however, believed that his virtues were complicated by self-deception and doubtful principle. In sixteenth-century views of history the conspiracy

*Editor's title. From *Unity in Shakespearian Tragedy* by Brents Stirling (New York: Columbia University Press, 1956).

against Caesar often represented a flouting of unitary sovereignty, that prime point of Tudor policy, and exemplified the anarchy thought to accompany "democratic" or constitutional checks upon authority. Certain judgments of Elizabethan political writers who refer to Brutus are quite clear upon this point. Although naturally aware of his disinterested honor and liberality, contemporary audiences could thus perceive in him a conflict between questionable goals and honorable action, a contradiction lying in his attempt to redeem morally confused ends by morally clarified means. The Elizabethan tragedy of Brutus, like that of Othello, is marked by an integrity of conduct which leads the protagonist into evil and measures him in his error.

When a dramatist wishes to present an idea, his traditional method, of course, is to settle upon an episode in which the idea arises naturally but vividly from action and situation. Such an episode in *Julius Caesar* is the one in which Brutus resolves to exalt not only the mission but the tactics of conspiracy: having accepted republicanism as an honorable end, he sets out to dignify assassination, the means, by lifting it to a level of rite and ceremony. In Act II, Sc. 1, as Cassius urges the killing of Antony as a necessary accompaniment to the death of Caesar, Brutus declares that "such a course will seem too bloody . . .,/To cut the head off and then hack the limbs." With this thought a sense of purpose comes over him: "Let's be sacrificers, but not butchers, Cassius." Here his conflict seems to be resolved, and for the first time he is more than a reluctant presence among the conspirators as he expands the theme which ends his hesitation and frees his moral imagination:

> We all stand up against the spirit of Caesar,
> And in the spirit of men there is no blood;
> Oh, that we then could come by Caesar's spirit,
> And not dismember Caesar! But, alas,
> Caesar must bleed for it! And, gentle friends,
> Let's kill him boldly, but not wrathfully;
> Let's carve him as a dish fit for the gods,
> Not hew him as a carcass fit for hounds.

This proposed conversion of bloodshed to ritual is the manner in which an abstract Brutus will be presented in terms of concrete art. From the suggestion of Plutarch that Brutus' first error lay in sparing Antony, Shakespeare moves to the image of Antony as a limb of Caesar, a limb not to be hacked because hacking is no part of ceremonial sacrifice. From Plutarch's description of Brutus as high-minded, gentle and disinterested, Shakespeare proceeds to the Brutus of symbolic action. Gentleness and disinterestedness become embodied in the act of "unwrathful" blood sacrifice. High-mindedness becomes objectified in ceremonial observance.

A skeptical reader may ask why the episode just described is any more significant than a number of others such as Brutus' scene with Portia or his quarrel with Cassius. If more significant, it is so only because of its relation to a thematic design. I agree, moreover, that Shakespeare gains his effects by variety; as a recognition, in fact, of his complexity I hope to show that the structure of *Julius Caesar* is marked by reference both varied and apt to Brutus' sacrificial rite, and that this process includes expository preparation in earlier scenes, emphasis upon "mock-ceremony" in both earlier and later scenes, and repeated comment by Antony upon butchery under the guise of sacrifice — ironical comment which takes final form in the parley before Philippi.

Derived in large measure from Plutarch, but never mechanically or unselectively, the theme of incantation and ritual is thus prominent throughout *Julius Caesar*, and this is no less true at the beginning than during the crucial episodes of Acts II and III. In the opening scene of the play we are confronted with a Roman populace rebuked by Marullus for ceremonial idolatry of Caesar:

> And do you now put on your best attire?
> And do you now cull out a holiday?
> And do you now strew flowers in his way
> That comes in triumph over Pompey's blood?

For this transgression Marullus prescribes a counter-observance by the citizens in immediate expiation of their folly:

> Run to your houses, fall upon your knees,
> Pray to the gods to intermit this plague
> That needs must light on this ingratitude.

To which Flavius adds:

> Go, go, good countrymen, and for this fault,
> Assemble all the poor men of your sort;
> Draw them to Tiber banks, and weep your tears
> Into the channel, till the lowest stream
> Do kiss the most exalted shores of all.

And after committing the populace to these rites of atonement for their festal celebration of Caesar, the two tribunes themselves leave to remove the devotional symbols set up for his welcoming. "Go you . . . towards the Capitol;/This way will I. Disrobe the images/If you do find them decked with ceremonies./. . . let no images/Be hung with Caesar's trophies." It is the hope of Flavius that these disenchantments will make Caesar "fly an ordinary pitch,/Who else would soar above the view of men."

104

Act I, Scene 2 is equally unusual in carrying the theme of ritual. It is apparent that Shakespeare had a wide choice of means for staging the entry of Caesar and his retinue; yet he selects an entry based upon Plutarch's description of the "feast Lupercalia" in which the rite of touching or striking barren women by runners of the course is made prominent. Caesar, moreover, after ordering Calpurnia to be so touched by Antony, commands: "Set on; and leave no ceremony out." It can be said, in fact, that the whole of this scene is written with ceremonial observance as a background. Its beginning, already described, is followed by a touch of solemnity in the soothsayer's words; next comes its main expository function, the sounding of Brutus by Cassius, and throughout this interchange come at intervals the shouts and flourishes of a symbolic spectacle. When the scene is again varied by a formal reentry and exit of Caesar's train, Casca remains behind to make a mockery of the rite which has loomed so large from off-stage. Significantly, in Casca's travesty of the ceremonial crown-offering and of the token offering by Caesar of his throat for cutting, Shakespeare has added a satirical note which does not appear in Plutarch.

The process, then, in each of the two opening episodes has been the bringing of serious ritual into great prominence, and of subjecting it to satirical treatment. In the first scene the tribunes denounce the punctilio planned for Caesar's entry, send the idolatrous crowd to rites of purification, and set off themselves to desecrate the devotional images. In the second scene a multiple emphasis of ceremony is capped by Casca's satire which twists the crown ritual into imbecile mummery. At this point, and in conformity with the mood set by Casca, occurs Cassius' mockery in soliloquy of Brutus:

> Well, Brutus, thou art noble; yet I see
> Thy honorable mettle may be wrought
> From that it is dispos'd; therefore it is meet
> That noble minds keep ever with their likes;
> For who is so firm that cannot be seduc'd?

The next scene (Act I, Sc. 3) is packed with omens and supernatural portents, a note which is carried directly into Act II, Sc. 1 where Brutus, on receiving the mysterious papers which have been left to prompt his action, remarks,

> The exhalations whizzing in the air
> Give so much light that I may read by them.

Appropriately, the letters read under this weird glow evoke his first real commitment to the "cause:"

> O Rome, I make thee promise

If the redress will follow, thou receivest
Thy full petition at the hand of Brutus!

Now appear his lines on the interim "between the acting of a dreadful thing/And the first motion" in which "the state of man/Like to a little kingdom, suffers then/The nature of an insurrection." This conventional symbolizing of political convulsion by inward insurrection is followed by the soliloquy on conspiracy:

O, then by day
Where wilt thou find a cavern dark enough
To mask thy monstrous visage? Seek none, Conspiracy!
Hide it in smiles and affability.

The conflict within Brutus thus becomes clear in this scene. First, the participant in revolution suffers revolution within himself; then the hater of conspiracy and lover of plain dealing must call upon Conspiracy to hide in smiling courtesy.

We have now reached the critical point (Act II, Sc. 1, 154ff.) to which attention was first called, an outward presentation of Brutus' crisis through his acceptance of an assassin's role upon condition that the assassins become sacrificers. Already a theme well established in preceding scenes, the idea of ritual is again made prominent. As the soliloquy on conspiracy closes, the plotters gather, and the issue becomes the taking of an oath. Brutus rejects this as an idle ceremony unsuited to men joined in the honesty of a cause and turns now to the prospect of Caesar's death. This time, however, honorable men do need ceremony, ceremony which will purify the violent act of all taint of butchery and raise it to the level of sacrifice. But although Brutus has steadied himself with a formula his conflict is still unresolved, for as he sets his course he "unconsciously" reveals the evasion which Antony later will amplify: to transmute political killing into ritual is to cloak it with appearances. We began with Brutus' passage on carving Caesar as a dish for the gods; these are the lines which complete it:

And let our hearts, as subtle masters do,
Stir up their servants to an act of rage,
And after seem to chide 'em. This shall make
Our purpose necessary and not envious;
Which so appearing to the common eyes,
We shall be called purgers, not murderers.

The contradiction is interesting. In an anticlimax, Brutus has ended his great invocation to ritual with a note on practical politics: our hearts shall stir us and afterward seem to chide us; we shall thus "appear" to the citizenry as purgers, not murderers.

Shakespeare never presents Brutus as a demagogue, but there are ironical traces of the politician in him which suggest Covell's adverse picture of Roman liberators. It is curious, in fact, that although Brutus is commonly thought to be unconcerned over public favor, he expresses clear concern for it in the passage just quoted and in Act III, Sc. 1, 244-51, where he sanctions Antony's funeral speech only if Antony agrees to tell the crowd that he speaks by generous permission, and only if he agrees to utter no evil of the conspiracy. Nor is Brutus' speech in the Forum wholly the nonpolitical performance it is supposed to be; certainly Shakespeare's Roman citizens are the best judges of it, and they react tempestuously. Although compressed, it scarcely discloses aloofness or an avoidance of popular emotive themes.

Act II, Scene 2 now shifts to the house of Caesar, but the emphasis on ritual continues as before. With dramatic irony, in view of Brutus' recent lines on sacrificial murder, Caesar commands, "Go bid the priests do present sacrifice." Calpurnia who has "never stood on ceremonies" (omens) is now terrified by them. News comes that the augurers, plucking the entrails of an offering, have failed to find a heart. Calpurnia has dreamed that smiling Romans have laved their hands in blood running from Caesar's statue, and Decius Brutus gives this its favorable interpretation which sends Caesar to his death.

The vivid assassination scene carries out Brutus' ritual prescription in dramatic detail, for the killing is staged with a formalized approach, ending in kneeling, by one conspirator after another until the victim is surrounded. This is met by a series of retorts from Caesar ending in "Hence! Wilt thou lift up Olympus," and the "sacrifice" is climaxed with his "Et tu Brute!" The conspirators ceremonially bathe their hands in Caesar's blood, and Brutus pronounces upon "this our lofty scene" with the prophecy that it "shall be acted over/In states unborn and accents yet unknown!"

The mockery in counterritual now begins as a servant of Antony enters (Act III, Sc. 1, 121) and confronts Brutus:

Thus, Brutus, did my master bid me kneel,
Thus did Mark Antony bid me fall down;
And being prostrate, thus he bade me say:
Brutus is noble, wise, valiant, and honest.

Here a threefold repetition, "kneel," "fall down," and "being prostrate," brings the ceremonial irony close to satire. Following this worship of the new idol by his messenger, Antony appears in person and with dramatic timing offers himself as a victim. In one speech he evokes both the holy scene which the conspirators so desired and the savagery which underlay it:

Now, whilst your purpled hands do reek and smoke,
Fulfill your pleasure. Live a thousand years,

> I shall not find myself so apt to die;
> No place will please me so, no mean of death,
> As here by Caesar, and by you cut off.

The murder scene is thus hallowed by Antony in a manner which quite reverses its sanctification by the conspirators. Brutus, forbearing, attempts to mollify Antony with his cherished theme of purgation:

> Our hearts you see not. They are pitiful,
> And pity to the general wrong of Rome —
> As fire drives out fire, so pity pity —
> Hath done this deed on Caesar.

Antony's response is again one of counterceremony, the shaking of hands in formal sequence which serves to make each conspirator stand alone and unprotected by the rite of blood which had united him with the others. The assassins had agreed as a token of solidarity that each of them should stab Caesar. Antony seems to allude to this:

> Let each man render me his bloody hand.
> First, Marcus Brutus, will I shake with you;
> Now, Caius Cassius, do I take your hand;
> Now. Decius Brutus, yours; now yours, Metellus;
> Yours, Cinna; and, my valiant Casca, yours;
> Though last, not least in love yours, good Trebonius.
> Gentlemen all — alas what shall I say?

It is then that Antony, addressing the body of Caesar, suddenly delivers this first profanation of the ritual sacrifice:

> Here wast thou bay'd brave hart;
> Here didst thou fall; and here thy hunters stand,
> Sign'd in thy spoil, and crimson'd in thy lethe.

And lest the allusion escape, Shakespeare continues Antony's inversion of Brutus' ceremonial formula: the dish carved for the gods is doubly transformed into the carcass hewn for hounds with further hunting metaphors of Caesar as a hart in the forest and as "a deer strucken by many princes." Brutus agrees to give reasons why Caesar was dangerous, "or else were this a savage spectacle," and the stage is set for what may be called the play's chief counterritual. Only Brutus, who planned the rite of sacrifice, could with such apt irony arrange the "true rites" and "ceremonies" which are to doom the conspiracy.

> I will myself into the pulpit first
> And show the reason of our Caesar's death.

What Antony shall speak, I will protest
He speaks by leave and by permission,
And that we are contented Caesar shall
Have all true rites and lawful ceremonies.

But exactly after the manner of his speech announcing the ritual sacrifice (Act II, Sc. 1) Brutus concludes again on a note of policy: "It shall advantage more than do us wrong."

Next follows Antony *solus* rendering his prophecy of "domestic fury and fierce civil strife" symbolized in Caesar's ghost which will

Cry "Havoc," and let slip the dogs of war,
That this foul deed shall smell above the earth.

The passage is similar in utterance, function, and dramatic placement to Carlisle's prophecy on the deposition of Richard II, and for that reason it is to be taken seriously as a choric interpretation of Caesar's death. Significantly, the beginning lines again deride Brutus' erstwhile phrase, "sacrificers but not butchers":

O, pardon me, thou bleeding piece of earth,
That I am meek and gentle with these butchers!

It is unnecessary to elaborate upon the Forum scene; Antony's oration follows the speech of Brutus with consequences familiar to all readers. But there is an element in Antony's turning of the tables which is just as remarkable as the well-known irony of his references to "honorable men." If we remember that Shakespeare has emphasized ritual at various planes of seriousness and of derision, the conclusion of Antony's speech to the populace will link itself with the previous theme. For here Antony reenacts the death of Caesar in a ritual of his own, one intended to show that the original "lofty scene" presented a base carnage. Holding Caesar's bloody mantle as a talisman, he reproduces *seriatim* the sacrificial strokes, but he does so in terms of the "rent" Casca made and the "cursed steel" that Brutus plucked away with the blood of Caesar following it. Again, each conspirator had struck individually at Caesar and had symbolically involved himself with the others; for the second time Antony reminds us of the ritual bond by recounting each stroke, and his recreation of the rite becomes a mockery of it. Brutus' transformation of blood into the heady wine of sacrifice is reversed both in substance and in ceremony.

For the "realists" among the conspirators what has occurred can be summed up in the bare action of the play: the killing of Caesar has been accomplished, but the fruits of it have been spoiled by Brutus' insistence that Antony live and that he speak at Caesar's funeral. "The which," as North's Plutarch has it "marred all." With reference to Brutus, however, something much more significant has been enacted; the "insurrection," the contradiction, within him has taken outward form in his attempt to purify assassination through ceremony. This act, not to be found in Plutarch, symbolizes the "Elizabethan" Brutus compelled by honor to join with conspirators but required by conscience to reject Conspiracy.

We have followed the ritual theme in *Julius Caesar* from early scenes to the point of Antony's oration, at which it is completely defined. There remains, however, a terminal appearance of the theme in the first scene of Act V. The ultimate clash between the idealism of Brutus and Antony's contempt for it comes during the parley on the eve of Philippi, at which Antony again drives home the old issue of ceremonial imposture. Brutus has observed that his enemy wisely threats before he stings; the reply is Antony's last disposition of the sacrificial rite:

> Villains, you did not so when your vile daggers
> Hack'd one another in the sides of Caesar,
> You show'd your teeth like apes, and fawn'd like hounds,
> And bow'd like bondmen, kissing Caesar's feet;
> Whilst damned Casca, like a cur, behind
> Struck Caesar on the neck.

Antony invokes the "hacking" which Brutus earlier foreswore, and he again inverts the cherished formula of sacrifice: once more the dish carved for gods becomes the carcass hewn for hounds. Over the body of Caesar he had previously employed the hunting-hound figure ("Here wast thou bay'd, brave hart."); the apes, the hounds, and the cur of these lines complete his vengeful irony of metaphor.

What, finally, is to be inferred from Antony's concluding passage on "the noblest Roman of them all"? Commonly found there is a broad vindication of Brutus which would deny an ironical interpretation. When Antony's elegiac speech is read plainly, however, its meaning is quite limited: it declares simply that Brutus was the only conspirator untouched by envy, and that, in intention, he acted "in a general honest thought/And common good to all." The Elizabethan view of Brutus as tragically misguided is thus consistent with Antony's pronouncement that he was the only disinterested member of the conspiracy. But Brutus is not to be summed up in an epitaph; as the impersonal member of a conspiracy motivated largely by personal ends, he sought in a complex way to resolve his contradiction by depersonalizing, ritualizing, the means.

Shakespeare's achievement, however, is not confined to the characterization of a major figure, for we have seen that the ceremonial motive extends beyond the personality of Brutus into the structure of the play. Exposition stressing the idea of ritual observance leads to the episode in which Brutus formulates the "sacrifice," and clear resolution of the idea follows in event and commentary. Structural craftsmanship thus supplements characterization and the two combine, as in *Richard II*, to state the political philosophy implicit in the play.

*Shakespeare's Brutus

Shakespeare idealized Plutarch's Brutus, but not in the direction of his own Henry V. The Roman conspirator has become an exemplary gentleman, and the chief sign of this is his set of scruples. His imagination is indeed so selfless, and his consideration of other men so full and kind, as almost to smother his powers and render him inactive. He is not very much like Hamlet, whose inaction, if inaction it is, has its paradoxical dynamics. But he is a sober step in that direction — too sober for the kind of success his creator, with a nimble bound back into the northern scene, is next to achieve.

If Brutus is less interesting than Hamlet, if his internal complications diminish rather than exhibit his dramatic force, the principal reason may be that Shakespeare has kept himself too conscious of a remote Roman grandeur in the scene. In Plutarch he seems always to have recognized an artist whom it would be rash to change, but his respect for the biographer was in the present case perhaps too solemn. The accommodation of his style to an ancient and alien atmosphere is amazingly complete, and there is in *Julius Caesar* a perfection of form which even he will never surpass. But the accommodation is something of a tour de force, and the perfection is of that sort which limits rather than releases poetry. *Julius Caesar* is more rhetoric than poetry, just as its persons are more orators than men. They all have something of the statue in them, for they express their author's idea of antiquity rather than his knowledge of life. They have the clarity and simplicity of worked marble, and are the easiest of Shakespeare's people to understand if one expects everything from speeches, and if one is innocent of the distinction between men and public men. The characters of *Julius Caesar* are public men. Even Antony and Caesar are. But Shakespeare's deepest interest is in the private man. And though he tries to find that man in Brutus he does not do so, because he has already submitted Brutus, like everybody else in the play, to the smoothing and simplifying process of a certain style. This style is in its way wonderful, but the hero who follows Brutus will accomplish infinitely greater wonders in no style at all, or at any rate in none that can be named; unless its name is Shakespeare's English.

Julius Caesar is least notable among Shakespeare's better plays for the distinctions of its speech. All of its persons tend to talk alike; their training has been forensic and therefore uniform, so that they can say anything with both efficiency and ease. With Marullus's first speech in the opening scene the play swings into its style: a style which will make it appear that nobody experiences the least difficulty in saying what he thinks. The phrasing is invariably flawless from the oral point of view; the breathing is right; no thought is too long for order or too short for roundness. Everything is brilliantly and surely said; the effects are underlined, the i's are firmly dotted. Speeches have tangible outlines, like plastic objects, and the drift from one of

*Editors title. From *Shakespeare* by Mark Van Doren (New York: Holt, Rinehart & Winston, Inc., 1939).

them to another has never to be guessed, for it is clearly stated.

The characters are accomplished in all the practical arts of statement. Not merely in the Forum is Brutus an orator — "I pause for a reply" (Act III, Sc. 2, 37) — but in his private tent, quarreling with Cassius. Dryden admired the famous quarrel scene (Act IV, Sc. 3) because it was "masculine," and his admiration was sound; yet the epithet implies a limitation of effect. The thump and rap of the repartee remind us once more that public men are training their tongues against each other; the dialogue, for all its power, could do with some relief by way of things half said or never said. Brutus and Cassius say it all — with knowledge, too, of how it will be taken. Along with the rest here they are artists in declamation.

Rhetorical questions abound in *Julius Caesar*.

> Wherefore rejoice? What conquest brings he home?
> What tributaries follow him to Rome
> To grace in captive bonds his chariot-wheels? . . .
> And do you now put on your best attire?
> And do you now cull out a holiday?
> And do you now strew flowers in his way
> That comes in triumph over Pompey's blood? (Act I, Sc. 1, 37-56)

There they are piled in parallel formation, and this is frequently the case. Antony knows best the trick of letting them forth singly, with the force of simple assertion:

> Did this in Caesar seem ambitious? (Act III, Sc. 2, 95)

> You will compel me, then, to read the will? (Act III, Sc. 2, 161)

Portia, the public wife of a public man, goes so far as to answer one of hers:

> Is Brutus sick? . . .
>   No, my Brutus;
> You have some sick offence within your mind. (Act II, Sc. 1, 261-68)

But all in these various ways know how to ask them, and how not to pause for a reply unless the pause too will be effective.

So are they tutored in the music of monosyllables. No play of Shakespeare's has so many, so superbly used. The seasoned orator strings short words together as often as he can — for an effect of artlessness, of sincerity that only speaks right on, and also because there is a secret pleasure in demonstrating the discipline of his tongue. It takes skill to deliver monosyllables in an agreeable and natural rhythm, and a rhetorician likes nothing better than problems of skill. In *Julius Caesar* there may be in one place as many as thirty monosyllables together.

And when the fit was on him, I did mark
How he did shake — 'tis true, this god did shake. (Act I, Sc. 2, 120-21)

When went there by an age, since the great flood,
But it was fam'd with more than with one man?
When could they say, till now, that talk'd of Rome . . .

(Act I, Sc. 2, 152-54)

I will come home to you; or, if you will,
Come home to me, and I will wait for you.
I will do so; till then, think of the world. (Act I, Sc. 2, 309-11)

        What's to do?
A piece of work that will make sick men whole.
But are not some whole that we must make sick? (Act II, Sc. 1, 326-28)

        Let me know some cause,
Lest I be laugh'd at when I tell them so.
The cause is in my will; I will not come. (Act II, Sc. 2, 69-71)

If thou dost bend and pray and fawn for him,
I spurn thee like a cur out of my way. (Act III, Sc. 1, 45-46)

'T is good you know not that you are his heirs;
For, if you should, O, what would come of it! (Act III, Sc. 2, 150-51)

I pray you, sirs, lie in my tent and sleep;
It may be I shall raise you by and by. . . .
I will not have it so: lie down, good sirs. . . .
I know young bloods look for a time to rest. . . .
I will not hold thee long. If I do live,
I will be good to thee. (Act IV, Sc. 3, 246-66)

They may occur in orations or they may crop up in discourse; they may be
triumphs by the orator Antony —

But, as you know me all, a plain blunt man
That love my friend;

But here I am to speak what I do know;
And I must pause till it come back to me —

or they may be the last words of a dying man:

I kill'd not thee with half so good a will.

They may serve any purpose at the moment. But the purpose they serve at all times is to pour into the ear an unimpeded stream of eloquence, a smooth current of artful sound. And once again it is to be noted that monosyllables are no one speaker's monopoly. The craft is native to them all.

So is the loftier craft of framing superlatives, of condensing infinite compliment into a finite phrase. Antony, being the best orator, does best at this:

> With the most noble blood of all this world (Act III, Sc. 1, 156)

> The choice and master spirits of this age (Act III, Sc. 1, 163)

> Thou art the ruins of the noblest man
> That ever lived in the tide of times (Act III, Sc. 1, 256-57)

> This was the noblest Roman of them all. (Act V, Sc. 5, 68)

But the second best of Brutus is impressive:

> That struck the foremost man of all this world (Act IV, Sc. 3, 22)

> The last of all the Romans, fare thee well!
> It is impossible that ever Rome
> Should breed thy fellow. (Act V, Sc. 3, 99-101)

And again the gift is common to the cast.

Their voices are not differentiated then. Nor are their states of mind. Brutus anticipates Hamlet, Othello, Lear, and Macbeth when he soliloquizes concerning the disorder in his soul:

> Between the acting of a dreadful thing
> And the first motion, all the interim is
> Like a phantasma or a hideous dream.
> The Genius and the mortal instruments
> Are then in council; and the state of a man,
> Like to a little kingdom, suffers then
> The nature of an insurrection. (Act II, Sc. 1, 63-69)

This is fine, like everything else in *Julius Caesar*, but it is rotund and political and it was relatively easy for Brutus to say; nor is it impossible to imagine another man's saying it. It is not, like comparable speeches in the tragedies ahead, cut to the individual, and cut with so keen a knife that the individual is dissected in the process and seems to bleed his words. Brutus addresses us through a wrapping of rhetoric, of public speech. And this

114

wrapping is around the imageries of blood and sleep which are so prominent in the play — so prominent, and yet, if one remembers *Macbeth*, so remote from contact with us. The blood that smears the entire surface of *Macbeth* is physical; we see, feel, and smell it. Not so with Caesar's blood; it is "noble" and "costly" because Caesar was the foremost man of all the world, but it remains a metaphor, a political metaphor, distant from the experience of our senses. It may be significant that it can pour from Caesar's statue as well as from his body (Act II, Sc. 2, 76-79), and that when he falls at the base of Pompey's statue it too runs red. There is as much real blood in *Julius Caesar* as there is in stone. And Brutus, once more ancestor to Macbeth, cannot sleep. At home before the assassination, in his tent on the eve of battle, and facing death in his last hour, his lids are heavy, his bones want rest. Yet the fact is not ghastly as in the case of one who will murder Sleep itself, and whose resulting exhaustion will visit itself upon the audience. The fatigue of Brutus is the noble tiredness of a great man, and we respect it; but our pity for the sufferer is not tinged with fear. This is the noblest Roman of them all, and even in distress he keeps his distance.

In such an atmosphere Caesar has little chance to be himself, yet Shakespeare has permitted him to make the most of it. Caesar is not a noble Roman, not one of Plutarch's men. He is that rarity in the play, an Elizabethan personality; he is one of Shakespeare's men. While he lasts he reveals himself in his irregularity, not in his symmetry, in picturesqueness rather than in pose. His monosyllables — for he speaks them too — tell us that he is deficient in one of the senses:

> Come on my right hand, for this ear is deaf; (Act I, Sc. 2, 213)

that he changes his mind suddenly, with no reason given:

> He is a dreamer; let us leave him. Pass; (Act I, Sc. 2, 24)

> The cause is in my will; I will not come; (Act II, Sc. 2, 71)

and that he is inordinately vain:

> But there's but one in all doth hold his place.
> So in the world; . . . and that I am he. (Act III, Sc. 1, 65-70)

His enemies tell us that he has the falling sickness (Act I, Sc. 2, 256), that he is gullible to flattery (Act II, Sc. 1, 207-8), that he is superstitious grown of late and loves to be regaled with wondrous tales of unicorns, bears, lions, and elephants (Act II, Sc. 195-206). He appears, indeed, only in his singularity; and he appears but briefly before he falls at the hands of men so completely unlike him that the difference alone might pass as motive for their hatred. Their hatred is of a man not noble, a man who has not suppressed himself.

And for a similar reason they distrust Antony, who revels long o' nights (Act II, Sc. 2, 116) and whose orator's tongue flicks unfairly with the serpent speed of irony. They cannot cope with his irony; it is a thing to which solemn men feel superior, and so, since they are not only solemn but innocent it is a thrust they cannot parry. It is what destroys them, along with much mischance and the heaped mountain of their blunders. They never know him as we do; they do not hear him, for example, prick down the character of Lepidus with epigrams as merciless as bullets (Act IV, Sc. 1). They never know the force that is coiled behind his charm. Nor do we know it as we shall in *Antony and Cleopatra*. But it is here, if only briefly as in the case of the eccentric Caesar.

The blunders of Brutus and Cassius, but particularly of Brutus, are many and pathetic. If they do not achieve the dignity of tragic error, of heroic fault, the trouble is with the men who make them; their virtues are not positive enough. This is less true of Cassius, who misconstrues everything at Philippi and so brings on the catasrophe (Act V, Sc. 3, 84). Throughout the play he has been the sharper figure. Caesar defines him in negative terms — "he hears no music" and "loves no plays" as Antony does, and "seldom he smiles" (Act I, Sc. 2, 203-5) — and yet it is from the same source that we learn something we never forget: "a lean and hungry look . . . such men are dangerous." His voice is lean and hungry too, as his mind is rank and practical; when Brutus sees Antony after the assassination he thinks of nothing but assuring him of his "kind love, good thoughts, and reverence," whereas Cassius is only waiting till he can ask:

But what compact mean you to have with us? (Act III, Sc. 1, 215)

Brutus has no patience with the poet who sneaks in at Philippi:

What should the wars do with these jigging fools?

But Cassius rasps out an angrier rebuke:

Ha, ha! how vilely doth this cynic rhyme! (Act IV, Sc. 3, 133)

He is the angrier of the two when they quarrel, and therefore he is dramatically the more interesting. He has more flaws than Brutus, who indeed has none except the dramatic one of an impenetrable and inexpressible nobility.

The mistakes of Brutus are the mistakes of a man whose nobility muffles his intelligence. His conquest of himself has extended to his wit; his excellence is not inconsistent with a certain lethargy of mind. He knows this well enough:

I am not gamesome; I do lack some part
Of that quick spirit that is in Antony. (Act I, Sc. 2, 28-29)

His honesty is absolute and disarming, so that he will not wait as Cassius does for Caesar to compare him unfavorably with the one brilliant person of the play. But honesty in him is humorless and edgeless; it rings a little dully in our ears, and even a little smugly:

> There is no terror, Cassius, in your threats,
> For I am arm'd so strong in honesty
> That they pass by me as the idle wind,
> Which I respect not. (Act IV, Sc. 3, 66-69)

He would not call this boasting; he would call it the truth, as indeed it is; but the fact that it is, and that he is the speaker, tells us everything about him. Neither would he admit that his behavior to Messala when Messala brings him the news of Portia's death is a piece of acting.

> *Brutus*: Now, as you are a Roman, tell me true.
> *Messala*: Then like a Roman bear the truth I tell:
> For certain she is dead, and by strange manner.
> *Brutus*: Why, farewell, Portia. We must die, Messala.
> With meditating that she must die once,
> I have the patience to endure it now.
> *Messala*: Even so great men great losses should endure.
> *Cassius*: I have as much of this in art as you,
> But yet my nature could not bear it so.
> *Brutus*: Well, to our work alive. What do you think
> Of marching to Philippi presently? (Act IV, Sc. 3, 187-97)

He would call it a demonstration of how Stoic gentlemen should conduct themselves. And in truth it is. Brutus already knows of Portia's death, for we have heard him telling Cassius of it. Cassius then is assisting him in the act, and Messala is being impressed as he should be. It is not vanity. It is virtue, it is true manhood demonstrating itself for the benefit of others. But to say as much is again to say that Brutus is humorlessly good. If his duty is to know himself, his performance fails. Nobility has numbed him until he cannot see himself for his principles. When his principles are expressing themselves they are beautiful in their clarity; his consideration for the tired boy Lucius is exquisite (Act IV, Sc. 3), and his last compliment to mankind should have been deserved:

> My heart doth joy that yet in all my life
> I found no man but he was true to me. (Act V, Sc. 5, 34-35)

But when he speaks to himself he knows not who is there; he addresses a strange audience, and fumbles. The reasoning with which he convinces himself that Caesar should be murdered is woefully inadequate.

> So Caesar may;
> Then, lest he may, prevent. (Act II, Sc. 1, 27-28)

The soliloquy of which these pitiful phrases are a part is riddled with rank fallacy. The fine man is a coarse thinker, the saint of self-denial has little self left to deny.

Shakespeare has done all that could be done with such a man, but what could be done was limited. The hero is heavy in the poet's hands; his reticence prevents intimacy, so that his blunders — as a conspirator with respect to Antony and as a general with respect to the time for attack — are difficult to excuse, they do not arouse in us any instinct to insist that to fail as such a man fails is to be glorious after all. Even the gentleness which will not let him desire Antony's death is in the last analysis confused. He is not mad, or haunted, or inspired, or perplexed in the extreme. He is simply confused. And the grounds of confusion in a man so negative are not to be known. Neither perhaps are they to be known in a man like Hamlet who uncovers something in himself with every word he utters. Yet we know the man — so well that his very attempts to evade us bring him closer. Hamlet may seldom mean what he says; and Shakespeare will never commit the error of exposing him in thought as he exposes Brutus; but we shall be instantly aware of what he means, at any rate to us, and we shall not fail to measure the disturbance in a too much changed mind.

*The Problem of *Julius Caesar*

Julius Caesar is one of Shakespeare's most perplexing plays. Its stylistic simplicity, coupled with an absence of bawdy lines, has made it a favorite school text, and this has led some critics to believe that it ought to be a simple play, a belief which has easily ripened into the conviction that it is a simple play. Others have acknowledged its perplexities. Professor Allardyce Nicoll calls it one of Shakespeare's "most difficult plays rightly to assess",[1] and Mr. Wilson Knight remarks that "to close analysis it reveals subtleties and complexities which render interpretation difficult."[2] There is widespread disagreement among critics about who is the play's principal character or whether it has a principal character, on whether it is a tragedy and if so whose, on whether Shakespeare wants us to consider the assassination as damnable or praiseworthy, while of all the chief characters in the play violently contradictory interpretations have been offered. To illustrate this polarity of views it will be sufficient to refer to two eminent critics. Professor Dover Wilson tells us that in this play Shakespeare adopted the traditional Renaissance view of Caesar, derived from Lucan, which regarded him as "a Roman Tamburlaine of illimitable ambition and ruthless irresistible genius; a monstrous tyrant who destroyed his country and ruined 'the mightiest and most flourishing commonwealth that the world will ever see.' "[3] "The

*By Ernest Schanzer, *Shakespeare Quarterly* VI (New York, 1955).

play's theme is the single one, Liberty versus Tyranny'' (p. xxi). The assassination is wholly laudable, the conspirators are unselfish champions of freedom, while Brutus' tragedy consists in vain struggle against the destiny of Rome, which lies in the establishment of Caesarism (p. xxii).

When we turn from this to Sir Mark Hunter's interpretation of the play we are told that ''there can be no doubt that to Shakespeare's way of thinking, however much he extends sympathy to the perpetrators of the deed, the murder of Julius was the foulest crime in secular history.'' Of Caesar we learn, ''When put to the test of the stage the personality of Julius 'moves before us as something right royal', a character sufficiently great to render the impassioned eulogy of Antony and the calm tribute of Brutus not inconsistent with what we have actually heard and seen of the object of their praise.'' Of the conspirators we are told, ''Brutus excepted, there is no sign anywhere that the enemies of the Dictator, though they have all the political catchwords at command — Liberty, Enfranchisement, etc. — care one jot for the welfare of any one outside their own order.'' And of Brutus, ''Noble-hearted and sincere beyond question, Brutus is intellectually dishonest'', he is self-righteous, pathetically inconsistent, a ''befogged and wholly mischievous politician.''[4]

Thus, while Dover Wilson roots the play in the dominant literary tradition of the Renaissance, which is overwhelmingly hostile to Caesar, Sir Mark Hunter, with equal confidence, places it in the dominant medieval tradition, which is wholly eulogistic. In this he is supported by so great an authority as W. W. Fowler, who tells us that Shakespeare's idea of Caesar ''was simply an inheritance from the education of the Middle Ages'', when the textbook for Roman History was that of Orosius, who brings out the greatness and moderation of Caesar and the cruel injustice of the assassination.[5] The reader of Shakespeare's play is thus faced with a difficult choice. Is he to throw in his lot with Professor Dover Wilson and Cassius, and regard Shakespeare's Caesar as a boastful tyrant, strutting blindly to his well-merited doom, and the assassination as a glorious act of liberation, or is he to follow Sir Mark Hunter and Mark Antony, and look at him as ''the noblest man that ever lived in the tide of times'', and at the assassination as a hideous crime? Fortunately for the less resolute spirits there is a third tradition in relation to which the play may be viewed, made up of writers whose reaction to Caesar and the conspiracy is not simple and undivided, like that of Lucan and Orosius, but of a complex and sometimes bafflingly contradictory nature.

Among these writers are above all Plutarch, Shakespeare's main source; Appian, with whose Roman History Shakespeare was probably acquainted in the 1578 translation; Suetonius; Dante; and a number of Renaissance writers, among them the author of the anonymous play entitled *Caesar's Revenge*, which, as I have argued elsewhere,[6] was probably one of the chief formative influences upon Shakespeare's play. The reasons for their divided attitude to the Caesar story vary, of course, a good deal among the different writers.

With Plutarch it seems to result largely from a personal dislike of Caesar's character, coupled with a belief in him as the Man of Destiny "whom God had ordained of special grace to be Governor of the Empire of Rome, and to set all things again at quiet stay, the which required the counsel and authority of an absolute Prince."[7] And much the same seems to me to hold true of Dante's attitude. Plutarch's view of the conspirators is also complicated by a desire to show "his angel" Brutus as the only just man among the wicked, joined with a reluctance to accept the conclusion that Brutus chose other than honest men for his associates. Plutarch is thus driven to alternate between blackening and whitewashing the character of Brutus' fellow-conspirators. Appian's divided attitude seems to arise mainly from a mingling of admiration for Brutus and Cassius, "two most noble and illustrious Romans, and of incomparable virtue, but for one crime", and an abhorrence of their foul deed of murder. "Yet by these men the act against Caesar was done, contrary in all thing, being no simple work, nor in no small matter, for it was against their friend, contrary to reason, and against their well doer, unthankfully, whom he had saved in the war, and against the chief ruler, injustly in the Senate house, and against an holy man, having on an holy vesture; and such an officer, as never was the like, so profitable to all men and to his country and Empire. The which God did punish in them, and many times gave tokens of it."[8] (Had Shakespeare this passage at the back of his mind when he made Macbeth, contemplating the murder of Duncan, recoil at the threefold violation of sacred relationships, that of kinsman, subject, and host, and declare that Duncan had been

> So clear in his great office, that his virtues
> Will plead like angels, trumpet-tongued, against
> The deep damnation of his taking-off (Act I, Sc. 7, 1866.)?)

The divided attitude in *Caesar's Revenge* issues largely from the author's attempt to combine Appian's presentation of the Caesar story, which seems to have served as his chief source, with that of the French Senecan plays of Muret, Garnier, and Grévin, which makes him both depict Caesar as a thrasonical, infatuated world-conqueror, and show Brutus driven to despair and suicide through the burden of guilt incurred by having murdered his friend and benefactor.

It is to this tradition of a divided, complex, and often ambiguous response to the Caesar story that Shakespeare's play belongs. But with Shakespeare, as I hope to show, this ambiguity and divided response, however much it may also be a reflection of his own feelings, is used as a deliberate dramatic device, and is no mere accidental inheritance from his sources. It seems highly likely that Shakespeare's own attitude to the Caesar story underwent a complete change as a result of his reading of Plutarch. His earlier response appears to have been much like that of his medieval ancestors and was probably also that of the great mass of the people of England who had heard of Caesar at all. To them he was one of the Nine Worthies, the great warrior hero, and his murderers were damnable villains. This view is above all expressed in the *Henry VI* plays.

> A far more glorious star thy soul will make
> Than Julius Caesar or bright —

Bedford says of the dead Henry V (*1 Henry VI*, Act I, Sc. 1, 49):

> They that stabb'd Caesar shed no blood at all,
> Did not offend, nor were not worthy blame,
> If this foul deed were by to equal it

Queen Margaret exclaims at the murder of her son (*3 Henry VI*, Act V, Sc. 5, 53); while Suffolk tells his assassins:

> Great men oft die by vile besonians:
> A Roman sworder and banditto slave
> Murder'd sweet Tully; Brutus' bastard hand
> Stabb'd Julius Caesar. (*2 Henry VI*, Act IV, Sc. 1, 137 ff.)

Added to this popular view of Caesar we find the knowledge of him as the writer of commentaries, a man of learning and wit. "Kent, in the commentaries Caesar wrote, Is term'd the civil'st place," we learn in *2 Henry VI*, Act IV, Sc. 7, 65. And in *Richard III* Prince Edward admiringly exclaims,

> That Julius Caesar was a famous man;
> With what his valour did enrich his wit,
> His wit set down to make his valour live:
> Death makes no conquest of this conqueror;
> For now he lives in fame, though not in life. (Act III, Sc. 1, 84 ff.)

After this the tone and content of the Caesar references change. In *As You Like It* Rosalind speaks jestingly of "Caesar's thrasonical brag of 'I came, saw, and overcame' ", and Falstaff makes a similar allusion at his capture of Coleville (*2 Henry IV*, Act IV, Sc. 3, 42). Cloten speaks of "Caesar's ambition Which swell'd so much that it did almost stretch The sides o' the world" (*Cymbeline*, Act III, Sc. 1, 49ff.). We hear no more of Caesar's valor, glory, or wit, but a good deal of his fabulous military skill (*All's Well*, Act III, Sc. 6, 56; *Othello*, Act II, Sc. 3, 127; *Cymbeline*, Act III, Sc. 1, 37). The references to Caesar and Brutus in the earlier plays are also of value in indicating what must have been the attitude to the Caesar story of at least a considerable portion of the audience. If the majority of the spectators at the performance of *3 Henry VI* had in fact felt that the murderers of Caesar "did not offend, nor were not worthy blame", Queen Margaret's comparison would, to say the least, be ill chosen. In the same way Bedford's hyperbole would be a mere lapse into bathos unless a large part of the audience were in sympathy with the medieval apotheosis of Caesar. But there must have been other members of the audience, readers of Lucan and Plutarch, who, a few years later, could respond to Shakespeare's sympathetic presentation of Brutus in *Julius Caesar*, without the interference of preconceptions about Brutus' bastard hand that stabbed his friend and benefactor. And there were probably others, readers of Plutarch, Appian, and Suetonius, who were divided in their attitude, and who had not made up their minds. It is this variety and division of views among his audience which, as it seems to me, Shakespeare deliberately exploited.

I propose to begin with a discussion of Shakespeare's presentment of the character of Caesar. Its nature will be seen most clearly by being rapidly followed scene by scene, from the opening of the play until Antony's funeral oration.

In Flavius and Marullus we get our first glimpses of the republican opposition to Caesar's rule. Loyalty to Pompey's memory as well as fear of future oppression seem their chief motives. The metaphor which Flavius uses to justify their "disrobing" of Caesar's images strikes an ominous note:

These growing feathers plucked from Caesar's wing
Will make him fly an ordinary pitch,
Who else would soar above the view of men
And keep us all in servile fearfulness. (Act I, Sc. 1, 76 ff.)

It points forward to the image of the serpent's egg applied to Caesar in Brutus' soliloquy. There a more drastic operation is advocated, but in both cases the action is thought of as preventive, directed not against what Caesar is but what he may become if not checked in time. Both images are probably indebted to a passage in Plutarch's "Life of Caesar", where his favorite equestrian metaphor is used to convey the same thought: "But in fine, when they had thus given him the bridle to grow to this greatness, and that they could not then pull him back, though indeed in sight it would turn one day to the destruction of the whole state and commonwealth of Rome: too late they found, that there is not so little a beginning of anything, but continuance of time will soon make it strong, when through contempt there is no impediment to hinder the greatness."[9] Immediately upon Flavius' words Caesar makes his first appearance, and the imaginative impact of this short scene tends to bear out rather than to discredit Flavius' fears. With the utmost economy of words Shakespeare manages to create the atmosphere of an oriental court with its cringing attendants and fawning favourites. "Peace, ho! Caesar speaks." "When Caesar says 'do this' it is performed." And into this atmosphere intrudes the first of the many warnings that come ever thicker as the moment of the murder approaches, and like all the others it is contemptuously brushed aside by Caesar. "He is a dreamer, let us leave him: pass."

From this slow-moving and portentous scene we pass at once to the rapid, feverish, and impassioned utterances of Cassius in his great seduction-scene. The contrast which Cassius draws between Caesar's physical defects, which make him succumb in a swimming-match and shake when suffering from a fever-fit, and the greatness of his position, is part of a general contrast, pervading the whole play, between Caesar's frailties of body and character and the strength of his spirit which has enabled him to become "the foremost man of all the world." Cassius is genuinely perplexed by this contrast. He is like a schoolboy who is puzzled and angry that someone whom he has always beaten at games should have become prefect and exact obedience from his physical equals and superiors.

> Now, in the names of all the gods at once,
> Upon what meat doth this our Caesar feed,
> That he is grown so great?

Contrary to his intention, Cassius does not throw doubt on Caesar's courage, but unwittingly testifies to it. It is the fever-fit that makes Caesar shake, not the prospect of jumping into "the troubled Tiber chafing with her shores". The story of the swimming-match epitomizes the triumph of Caesar's daring and resolution over his physical frailties.

It is significant that in this crucial scene, where Cassius can be expected to make the most of the opposition's case against Caesar, he makes no mention of any specific acts of oppression or tyrannical behavior. There is only the general assertion that Rome is "groaning underneath this age's yoke". But the yoke to Cassius lies in one man's usurpation of the honors and powers that previously belonged to many. To him the yoke is therefore very much an existing reality, whereas to Brutus the threat lies not in present but in impending conditions.

> Brutus had rather be a villager
> Than to repute himself a son of Rome
> Under these hard conditions as this time
> Is like to lay upon us

he tells Cassius in this scene. And in his soliloquy it is again not what Caesar is but what he may become that causes his fears.

What, then, is the effect of this scene upon our mental picture of Caesar? It heightens, rather than alters, our previous impression of him as an oriental monarch, a Colossus, and begins the process, continuing through much of the play, of disjoining and contrasting the human and the superhuman Caesar, the man with his physical and moral frailties and the God who is beyond human frailties. Caesar, by constantly putting himself outside the pale of humanity, collaborating, as Mr. John Palmer so well puts it,[10] in his own deification, yet reminding us of his frailties on each of his appearances, underlines this dissociation. In the very next episode we find him angry at the mob's opposition to his acceptance of the crown, afraid of Cassius, yet assuring Antony

> I rather tell thee what is to be feared
> Than what I fear; for always I am Caesar..

And at once follows the body-spirit contrast:

> Come on my right hand, for this ear is deaf
> And tell me truly what thou think'st of him (Act I, Sc. 2, 211)

As Dover Wilson points out (p. 113), the atmosphere is again that of the oriental court. When Caesar is angry "all the rest look like a chidden train." In his remarks about Cassius we get our chief glimpse of the Caesar we know from Plutarch, the shrewd politician, the keen observer of men, the Caesar of the Commentaries.

In Casca's narration of the day's events a new Caesar is revealed to us, again with Plutarchian traits, Caesar the play-actor, skilfully exploiting the passions of the mob. While his fall in the market place is a sort of preview of his later fall in the Capitol, his adroit play upon the feelings of the mob adumbrates Antony's manipulation of them in his funeral oration. Casca's report ends on an ominous note, which, for the moment, makes the worst fears of the enemies of Caesar seem justified: "Marullus and Flavius, for pulling scarfs off Caesar's images, are put to silence." Not deprived of their tribuneship, as in Plutarch, but simply, cryptically, "put to silence".

Up to this point Shakespeare has tipped the balance in favor of the conspirators' view of Caesar and has made us share Brutus' apprehensions. Now, by making Cassius, in his soliloquy, so frankly impugn the integrity of his own motives and show us so clearly the personal nature of his opposition, we are brought to question the truth of our impression of Caesar, so much of which we have received through Cassius. And our doubts are strengthened by the play's next image of Caesar, again drawn by Cassius, this time for the terrorstricken Casca. For Cassius' picture of Caesar and his explanation of the portents is clearly part of an *argumentum ad hominem*. Cassius himself is an Epicurean and does not, at least not yet, "credit things that do presage". But to convince Casca, who does credit them, of the monstrosity of Caesar's ru'e, he is quite ready to put them to use to prop up his arguments. Against Cassius' explanation of the omens we have been indirectly warned just before by Cicero:

> But men may construe things, after their fashion,
> Clean from the purpose of the things themselves.

The groundwork of Cassius' indictment of Caesar here is much the same as in his scene with Brutus. There is again the contrast between what Caesar really is and what he has become, but what he has become is something slightly different fitting the altered circumstances. It is no longer a God or a Colossus who dwarfs his fellowmen, and thus prevents them from achieving personal glory. This representation of Caesar seemed to Cassius suited to Brutus in whom he is trying to awake a sense of thwarted ambition. But upon the terrified Casca it is a sense of the fearfulness of Caesar that he tries to impress.

> Now could I, Casca, name to thee a man
> Most like this dreadful night,
> That thunders, lightens, opens graves, and roars
> As doth the lion in the Capitol;
> A man no mightier than thyself or me
> In personal action, yet prodigious grown
> And fearful, as these strange eruptions are. (Act I, Sc. 3, 72 ff.)

But while the picture of Caesar as a God and a Colossus bore some semblance to the reality of which we have been allowed a few glimpses, the Caesar that "thunders, lightens, opens graves, and roars" is too obviously a fabrication of the moment for argumentative purposes to affect our mental image of the man. The ironic fact that Caesar later seems to bear out Cassius' description by referring to himself as a lion and Danger's elder twin-brother does not alter this impression. For it is Caesar's most ludicrous utterance, and no more affrights us than Snug the joiner's impersonation of that "fearful wildfowl". Our image of Caesar receives its next modification in Brutus' soliloquy. Brutus' Caesar bears no resemblance either to Cassius' God and Colossus or to his roaring lion. He appears to Brutus in the image of a serpent's egg, someone yet harmless but potentially mischievous because of his desire for the crown. At the very moment when it is most in Brutus' interest to incriminate Caesar his intellectual honesty forces him to declare:

> And to speak truth of Caesar
> I have not known when his affections swayed
> More than his reason.

It is an echo of Plutarch's "And now for himself, after he had ended his Civil Wars, he did so honourably behave himself, that there was no fault to be found in him" ("Caesar", p. 86). But are we to take this as a valid estimate of Caesar's character? Or is it as mistaken as Brutus' view of Antony and Cassius? His reference to Caesar's "lowliness" suggests this, for it is ludicrously inapposite to what we see of Caesar in this play. Thus Shakespeare calls in doubt the validity of Brutus' image of Caesar, just as he calls in doubt Cassius' image, and later Antony's, so that the nature of the real Caesar remains an enigma.

Nor is this enigma dispelled by what we see of Caesar in the following scenes. Even in the privacy of his home he is strenuously engaged in the creation of the legendary Caesar. There is never any real intimacy in his scene with Calphurnia, no momentary lifting of the mask in a soliloquy or an aside. Here and in the Capitol Shakespeare gives us above all the thrasonical Caesar, who sees himself as outside and above humanity.

> Caesar shall forth: the things that threaten'd me
> Ne'er looked but on my back; when they shall see
> The face of Caesar, they are vanished.
> Of all the wonders that I yet have heard,
> It seems to me most strange that men should fear.
> . . . . Danger knows full well
> That Caesar is more dangerous than he:
> We are two lions littered in one day,
> And I the elder and more terrible.

Only upon the arrival of the conspirators does he unbend a little, for the first and last time in the play. For his bearing here Shakespeare is probably indebted to Plutarch's description of the youthful Caesar: "And the people loved him marvellously also because of the courteous manner he had to speak to every man, and to use them gently, being more ceremonious therein than was looked for in one of his years. Furthermore, he ever kept a good board, and fared well at his table, and was very liberal besides" ("Caesar", p. 5). Plutarch's coupling of Caesar's hospitality with his courtesy probably suggested to Shakespeare his

> Good friends, go in and taste some wine with me;
> And we, like friends, will straightway go together.

But these lines also call up memories of the ceremonial sharing of wine before another betrayal, memories which are strengthened by the kiss which Brutus gives to Caesar in the Capitol ("I kiss thy hand, but not in flattery, Caesar"), and later by Antony's reproach of Brutus at Philippi:

> In your bad strokes, Brutus, you give good words.
> Witness the hole you made in Caesar's heart
> Crying "Long live! hail Caesar!" (Act V, Sc. 1, 30 ff.)

("And forthwith he came to Jesus, and said, Hail master; and kissed him", Matthew xxvi. 49).

We are next given another estimation of Caesar and the conspiracy in Artemidorus'

My heart laments that virtue cannot live
Out of the teeth of emulation.
If thou read this, O Caesar, thou mayst live;
If not, the Fates with traitors do contrive.

Having engaged our sympathies for Caesar more fully than at any previous point in the play, Shakespeare loses little time to alienate them again, so that by the moment of the assassination our antipathies are more strongly aroused than ever before. In his two short speeches in the Capitol Shakespeare gives us a compendium of Caesar's most unamiable qualities: the cold, glittering hardness, the supreme arrogance, and again the dissociation of himself from the rest of mankind. A note of irony intrudes in his reference to his constancy:

But I am constant as the northern star,
Of whose true-fixed and resting quality
There is no fellow in the firmament.

The whole speech is ironic both in view of the mental vacillation which we have just witnessed, and his impending fall. It anticipates Othello's similarly ironic comparison of himself to the Pontic sea, which is equally belied by succeeding events. Shakespeare adds a final somewhat ludicrous touch in Caesar's "Hence! Wilt thou lift up Olympus?", which, juxtaposed with the immediately succeeding spectacle of his lifeless body lying at the foot of Pompey's statue, crystallizes the contrast between the corporeal and spiritual Caesar, which is summed up a little later by Antony's

O mighty Caesar! dost thou lie so low?
Are all thy conquests, glories, triumphs, spoils
Shrunk to this little measure? (Act III, Sc. 1, 149 ff.)

From Antony we now receive our last image of Caesar. His is the Caesar of popular medieval tradition, the great warrior, the Mirror of Knighthood, the noble Emperor. There is Caesar's nobility,

Thou art the ruins of the noblest man
That ever lived in the tide of times;
his fidelity,
He was my friend, faithful and just to me;
his largesse,
To every Roman citizen he gives,
To every several man, seventy five drachmas:
his military prowess,
He hath brought many captives home to Rome;
his compassionate nature,
When that the poor have cried, Caesar hath wept.

Yet though we are not made to doubt the sincerity of Antony's tribute to Caesar in his soliloquy, the image of him created by Antony in his funeral oration is called into question by its forming a part of Antony's consummate and carefully contrived play upon the emotions of the crowd. As with Cassius' and Brutus' image of Caesar, we cannot accept it as a simple presentment of facts.

Throughout the first half of the play, then, we are given a series of images of Caesar none of which bear much mutual resemblance, though some of them are not irrreconcilable with each other. There are the two Caesar's of Cassius, there is Casca's Caesar, Brutus' Caesar, Artemidorus' Caesar, and finally Antony's Caesar. But doubt is thrown in one way or another on the validity of most of these images. And to these Shakespeare adds his own presentation of Caesar, a presentation so enigmatic and ambiguous that none of the other images are really dispelled by it. It is a Pirandellian presentation of the Caesar figure. "Which of all these is the real Caesar?" Shakespeare seems to ask. And he takes care not to provide an answer. But does not Shakespeare further anticipate Pirandello by making us feel that perhaps there *is* no real Caesar, that he merely exists as a set of images in other men's minds and his own? For Shakespeare's Caesar is continuously engaged in what Pirandello calls *costruirsi*, "building himself up", creating his own image of Caesar, until we are left to wonder whether a lifting of the mask would reveal to us any face at all.

What reasons lie behind Shakespeare's peculiar presentation of the figure of Caesar? The usual answer given by critics, that Shakespeare draws Caesar unsympathetically in order to preserve our regard for the conspirators, or, as Bernard Shaw more bluntly put it, that he writes "Caesar down for the mere technical purpose of writing Brutus up",[11] will not do. For, as we have seen, what is involved in Shakespeare's presentation is something quite different from a mere writing down of the character. Another explanation is provided by Mr. H. M. Ayres who, as long ago as 1910, argued that, ever since Muret modelled his Caesar on the braggart Hercules of Seneca, the typical stage Caesar in the Renaissance was the vainglorious, hubristic figure of the French Senecans, and that Shakespeare had to endow his Caesar with these characteristics to fulfil the expectations of his audience.[12] However, there is no indication that any of the Elizabethan Caesar plays that were performed in the public theaters were influenced by the French Senecans. Muret, Grévin, and Garnier wrote only for academic audiences, and even a more popular play, like the anonymous *Caesar's Revenge*, may never have reached the public stage, for on its title-page appears the note, "Privately acted by the Studentes of Trinity College in Oxford". If Shakespeare endowed his Caesar with traits ultimately derived from the French Senecan Caesar plays he must have done so for other reasons than those suggested by Mr. Ayres.

Partly Shakespeare's presentment of Caesar was probably done in the interest of dramatic suspense. Shakespeare appears to be playing on the audience's divided attitude to the Caesar story, giving encouragement in turn to each man's preconceived ideas. And since on our estimate of Caesar depends to a large extent our view of the justification of the entire conspiracy, the whole drama is thus kept within the area of the problem-play. For though, as it seems to me, Shakespeare makes abundantly clear the catastrophic consequences of the murder, he does not, I think, make wholly clear its moral indefensibility. His ambiguous presentment of the Caesar figure allows responses like that of Professor Dover Wilson to be formulated, and I see no reason to doubt that there were also Dover Wilsons in Shakespeare's audience. In fact, the polarity of critical estimates of the character of the main *dramatis personae* and of the poet's attitude to the conspiracy bears witness to Shakespeare's success in making *Julius Caesar* a problem play. It is a problem play in much the same way as the *Wild Duck*, which has a very similar theme: the tragic mischief created by the actions of a young idealist in fulfilment of the highest principles, partly through his utter blindness to what people are really like. In both cases the question is put to the audience: "Was he or was he not morally justified in doing what he did?", and in both cases the dramatist's answer seems to me an insistent but not a compelling "No".

The main purpose of Shakespeare's dissociation of the corporeal and the spiritual Caesar throughout the play is, no doubt, to show up the futility and foolishness of the assassination. The whole second part of the play is an ironic comment on Brutus'

> We all stand up against the spirit of Caesar,
> And in the spirit of men there is no blood;
> O, that we then could come by Caesar's spirit,
> And not dismember Caesar! (Act II, Sc. 1, 169 ff.)

What is involved in the second half of the play is more than a grim pun, which makes the conspirators find that, while they have dismembered Caesar's body, his spirit, i.e. his ghost, still walks abroad, and exacts his revenge. For the spirit of Caesar is also that legendary figure, that God and Colossus, whom Cassius deplores, and whom Caesar seeks to impose upon the imagination of his countrymen and, it would seem, upon his own. In this he is handicapped by physical and moral frailties from which the murder frees him, and allows the legendary Caesar to come into his own, assisted by Antony's rhetoric, just as Antony later assists that other "spirit" of Caesar, his ghost, in executing his revenge.

That the spirit of Caesar in the sense of "Caesarism", the absolute rule of a single man, informs the second part of the play, as MacCallum, Dover Wilson, and others maintain, seems to me unsupported by anything in the text. Dover Wilson writes: "When Brutus exclaims 'We all stand up against the spirit of Caesar' he sums up the play in one line. For the spirit of Caesar, which was the destiny of Rome, is the fate against which Brutus struggles in vain" (p. xxii). And MacCallum, in a rather different spirit, tells us that

"Shakespeare makes it abundantly clear that the rule of the single master-mind is the only admissible solution for the problem of the time."[13] Both these critics, and the many others who have expressed similar opinions, seem to me to be reading Plutarch's view into Shakespeare's play. Nothing in the play suggests to me that Caesar is to be thought of as the Man of Destiny or that the establishment of one man's rule is the inevitable outcome of the Civil War. As in Plutarch, the people are shown to be strongly opposed to Caesar's assumption of the crown, as the Lupercal scene makes clear. Over against this can only be set the plebeians' shouts after Brutus' speech, "Let him be Caesar", "Caesar's better parts shall be crowned in Brutus", but to take these as evidence of strong monarchic feelings among the Roman people is surely to miss their function in the scene's context. At Philippi it is not Caesarism or the providential scheme of Plutarch and Dante which defeats Brutus and Cassius, but their flaws of soldiership and character, which make Brutus give the word for attack too early, and Cassius slay himself rashly, in premature despair. As far as the supernatural interferes in the affairs of men, it is Caesar's ghost rather than the hand of God that contributes to the defeat of the conspirators. Nor are we anywhere made to feel, as we are in Plutarch and Appian, that the Roman Republic has sunk into a state of corruption which only the establishment of one man's rule can cure.

Kittredge was undoubtedly right when, first among critics, he pointed to the element of "hubris" ... that pervades Shakespeare's portrayal of Caesar.[14] His infatuation, which makes him disregard all warnings, is repeatedly emphasized, from his first contemptuous dismissal of the sooth-sayer until his refusal to read Artemidorus' petition, and is pointed out by Calphurnia: "Alas, my lord, Your wisdom is consumed in confidence." His "hubris" is heightened with each appearance until it reaches its climax in his last speech in the Capitol. It is not difficult to trace the pedigree of this tragedy of "hubris," which is one of the several tragedies imbedded in the play. It is in a direct line of descent from Greek tragedy by way of Seneca, the adaptation of Senecan tragedy to the Caesar story by Muret and his imitators and its adoption in the *Caesar's Revenge* play. But while the theme of "hubris" is dominant in all the plays in the Muret tradition, that of blind infatuation is only developed by Shakespeare.

We have seen, then, that in *Julius Caesar* Shakespeare puts a twofold problem before his audience: There is the psychological problem of the nature of the real Caesar; and hinging upon it there is the ethical problem of the moral defensibility of the murder. Looked at in this way *Julius Caesar* reveals an unobtrusive kinship with Shakespeare's other chief problem-play, *Measure for Measure*. Central to both is a moral choice imposed upon the protagonists, Brutus and Isabel. And in both cases Shakespeare, while, as it seems to me, strongly suggesting by the orientation of his dramatic material the wrongfulness of their choice, makes it remain sufficiently problematic to allow his audience to form varying views about it.

[1]Allardyce Nicoll, *Shakespeare*, p. 134.
[2]G. Wilson Knight, *The Imperial Theme*, p. 63.
[3]*Julius Caesar* (New Cambridge edition), p. xxv.
[4]*Trans. Royal Soc. Lit.*, X (1931), 136 ff.
[5]W. W. Fowler, *Roman Essays and Interpretations*, p. 273.
[6]*Notes and Queries*, New Series, I, 5 (1954).
[7]*Tudor Translations*, ed. W. E. Henley, XII, 237. ("Comparison of Dion with Brutus"
[8]Appian, *Roman History*, 1578 translation, p. 303.
[9]P. 5. All page-references in the article are to *Shakespeare's Plutarch*, ed. Tucker Brooke, 2 vol., in the *Shakespeare's Library* series.
[10]John Palmer, *Shakespeare's Political Characters*, p. 37.
[11]G. B. Shaw, *Three Plays for Puritans* (Constable, 1925), p. xxx.
[12]*PMLA*, XXV. 183 ff.
[13]Sir Mungo MacCallum, *Shakespeare's Roman Plays*, p. 214.
[14]*Julius Caesar*, ed. Kittredge, *Introduction*.

Selected Criticisms

What attracted Shakespeare to this theme? And, first and foremost, what *is* the theme? The play is called *Julius Caesar*, but it was obviously not Caesar himself that attracted Shakespeare. The true hero of the piece is Brutus; he it is who has aroused the poet's fullest interest. We must explain to ourselves the why and wherefore. . . .

Shakespeare, having so arranged his drama that Brutus should be its tragic hero, had to concentrate his art on placing him in the foreground, and making him fill the scene. The difficulty was not to let his lack of political insight (in the case of Antony), or of practical sense (in his quarrel with Cassius), detract from the impression of his superiority. He had to be the centre and pivot of everything, and therefore Caesar was diminished and belittled to such a degree, unfortunately, that this matchless genius in war and statesmanship has become a miserable caricature. . . .

But here! here Caesar has become in effect no little of a braggart, and is compounded, on the whole, of anything but attractive characteristics. He produces the impression of an invalid. His liability to the "falling sickness" is emphasised. He is deaf of one ear. He has no longer his old strength. He faints when the crown is offered to him. He envies Cassius because he is a stronger swimmer. He is as superstitious as an old woman. He rejoices in flattery, talks pompously and arrogantly, boasts of his firmness and is for ever wavering. He acts incautiously and unintelligently, and does not realise what threatens him, while every one else sees it clearly.

George Brandes

Shakespeare is no partisan in this tragedy. He sides neither with Caesar and his avengers nor with the party of Brutus and Cassius. The verdict, if there must be a verdict, he leaves to history. Caesar, by the testimony of Brutus, was "the foremost man of all this world" (Act IV, Sc. 3, 22); Cassius, by the same testimony, was 'the last of all the Romans' (Act V, Sc. 3, 99); and the drama closes with a tribute to Brutus, "the noblest Roman of them all."

G. L. Kittredge

If Brutus is less interesting than Hamlet, if his internal complications diminish rather than exhibit his dramatic force, the principal reason may be that Shakespeare has kept himself too conscious of a remote Roman grandeur in the scene. *Julius Caesar* is more rhetoric than poetry, just as its persons are more orators than men. They all have something of the statue in them, for they express their author's idea of antiquity rather than his knowledge of life. They have the clarity and simplicity of worked marble, and are the easiest of Shakespeare's people to understand if one expects everything from speeches, and if one is innocent of the distinction between men and public men. The characters of *Julius Caesar* are public men. Even Antony and Caesar are. But Shakespeare's deepest interest is in the private man. And though he tries to find that man in Brutus he does not do so, because he has already submitted Brutus, like everybody else in the play, to the smoothing and simplifying process of a certain style. This style is in its way wonderful, but the hero who follows Brutus will accomplish infinitely greater wonders in no style at all, or at any rate in none that can be named; unless its name is Shakespeare's English.

Mark Van Doren

. . . A hero, let us be clear, is the character of which a dramatist, not morally, but artistically, most approves. Macbeth is a hero. Shakespeare's sympathy with Brutus does not imply approval of the murder of Caesar; it only means that he ultimately finds the spiritual problem of the virtuous murderer the most interesting thing in the story. Brutus best interprets the play's theme: Do evil that good may come, and see what does come! . . .

He (Shakespeare) is more interested, as he always has been, in character than in plot. He pays, goodness knows, small respect to the plots of the three contemporary comedies; they live by character alone. This, however, is history again, and plot must count. . . . His task now is less to elaborate or invent than to capture and transmit as much of such events and such men as his little London theater will hold. It is a feat of stagecraft to show us so many significant facets of this more than personal tragedy, a finer one to share out the best of the play's action among three chief characters and yet hardly lessen the strength of any of them.

Harley Granville-Barker

The main issue of the play is not the conspirators' fate but the future of Rome, of liberty, of the human race, to which their fate is incidental. Though Brutus is a tragic hero whom we pity, the heart of his tragedy is the defeat of his cause. His death is but a symbol of a greater disaster, the death of liberty. And the defeat is brought about, not at Philippi, but through the corruption and instability of human nature.

. . . When Brutus exclaims "We all stand up against the spirit of Caesar," he sums up the play in one line. For the spirit of Caesar, which was the destiny of Rome, is the fate against which Brutus struggles in vain. And his failure to do so is his tragedy (and ours), inasmuch as Caesarism is a secular threat to the human spirit, and the living 'Julius,' as Shakespeare shows him, is the mouthpiece of that threat.

John Dover Wilson

It is indeed difficult to discount entirely the muddle-headedness of Brutus, in spite of our national proclivity to condone the intellectual fuddles of a man whose heart intends good. But even the generous humanity of Shakespeare must have recoiled from a Brutus who desires the proceeds of wrongdoing but upbraids the other man for soiling his hands in getting them for him, as Brutus pharisaically rounds on Cassius when, at the request of Brutus, Cassius has found pay for Brutus' army by an illegal capital levy. There is, too, a suspicion of the Pharisee's smirk in Brutus' ideal recoil from conspiracy at the moment when he is about to welcome his fellow-conspirators. Neither is his conviction of assured intellectual superiority an engaging trait, when he puts aside the military dispositions of Cassius' more practical strategy. And these are broadly human obstacles to admiration. On the top of them, to Shakespeare, Brutus was politically a regicide in act, if not in name; and his own plea in claiming justifiable homicide was explicitly built on no more than a speculation about what the victim might possibly have aspired to. The victim, too, was one from whom he had himself enjoyed particular favour. Killing, surely, needs more excuse than this; and Brutus' murder of Caesar is a killing which excites faint or overt suspicions of murder, patricide and regicide linked in one dread deed.

H. B. Charlton

The study of the dramatic purposes for which language and imagery are used in *Julius Caesar* suggests solutions for the problems both of style and diction and of the nature and unity of the play. The imagery of words and action points to the imaginative and dramatic unity of the play as consisting in the completion of the circle of events beginning and ending the rebellion. The action of the play turns on the distance between the ideals and public symbols for which the names of Caesar, Brutus, and Cassius stand, and their true nature and actions. The three main figures are all noble and yet weak; none has the stature of hero or villain. Brutus and Cassius kill the man Caesar and not his spirit, not what he stands for, what they aim to destroy; it is a treacherous and dishonorable act which brings disorder, loss of the liberty they had sought, and finally civil war. All they had hoped to gain they lose, until they have nothing left but their names, and the opportunity to die bravely, to find freedom in suicide.

R. A. Foakes

Actually the play is full of submerged irony. On the surface, all is solemn, dignified, Roman. Even "thrasonical Caesar" boasts in high sentence and the style throughout comes closer to what Arnold would call sublime than almost any other play of Shakespeare's. But underneath are forces at work which seem to mock the dignity and sublimity. Numerous critics have noted, for example, that Brutus is as guilty in his way of hubris and delusions of infallibility as Caesar. This is attributed to the consciousness of his virtue. But what a curious virtue it is! He cannot stoop to bribetaking or extortion, but he becomes highly incensed when he is refused the money which Cassius has collected in this manner. In his last speech he proclaims himself satisfied with life for he had never met a man who was untrue to him, yet he, himself, has betrayed his best friend and he has in turn been betrayed by Antony. Even more ironic, perhaps, is the most celebrated speech of all, the "noblest Roman" speech. It is spoken of a man whom the same speaker only a hundred or so lines back has called to his face a hound, a flatterer and a traitor. And it is spoken in all earnestness; the characters themselves seem unaware of these discrepancies between the outer and the inner Roman.

Bernard Breyer

Partly Shakespeare's presentment of Caesar was probably done in the interest of dramatic suspense. Shakespeare appears to be playing on the audience's divided attitude to the Caesar story, giving encouragement in turn to each man's preconceived ideas. And since on our estimate of Caesar depends to a large extent our view of the justification of the entire conspiracy, the whole drama is thus kept within the area of the problem-play. For though, as it seems to me, Shakespeare makes abundantly clear the catastrophic consequences of the murder, he does not, I think, make wholly clear its moral indefensibility. . . .

We have seen, then, that in *Julius Caesar* Shakespeare puts a twofold problem before his audience: There is the psychological problem of the nature of the real Caesar; and hinging upon it there is the ethical problem of the moral defensibility of the murder. Looked at in this way *Julius Caesar* reveals an unobtrusive kinship with Shakespeare's other chief problem-play, *Measure for Measure*. Central to both is a moral choice imposed upon the protagonists, Brutus and Isabel. And in both cases Shakespeare, while . . . suggesting by the orientation of his dramatic material the wrongfulness of their choice, makes it remain sufficiently problematic to allow his audience to form varying views about it.

Ernest Schanzer

Caesar grows in stature as the play proceeds; Brutus deteriorates. In his quarrel with Cassius he is irritable, undignified, and unjust; he is more intolerant of the meddlesome poet than Cassius; and though he vehemently disputes Cassius's claim to be the abler soldier, his reasons for engaging the enemy at Philippi are less convincing than those of Cassius for deferring the battle. It is impossible to reconcile Shakespeare's presentation of Brutus with the common Renaissance view of him as the great liberator and . . . the second of his name to free the Romans from the tyrant's yoke.

T. S. Dorsch

134

The first of the two chief theses of the present interpretation is that the central quality of Brutus is not his virtue. It is his will. His virtue is the splendid muffling that clothes his will, that hides it from all cynical, envious eyes, that garbs a thoroughly egotistical willfulness in the white radiance of incorruptible principle. His virtue is his preoccupation, whence his unworldliness, and his virtue is his self-justification, whence his invariable insistence upon his own way. With his virtue he fools everyone, even himself. A close inspection of his lines shows that his will is the chief constant of his behavior, and that that will is impregnably fortified with his rock-solid belief in his own virtue. His strength is as the strength of ten because *he thinks* his heart is pure. This pattern was further enhanced by the fact that both friends (Act I, Sc. 3, 157-160; Act II, Sc. 1, 90-93) and enemies (Act V, Sc. 5, 68-77) took him at his own face value, reinforcing by look, gesture, and voice his own opinion of himself.

The second main thesis here is the Brutus' character is not a mystery, not something beyond anyone's — including Shakespeare's — comprehension, but instead is a presentation of the surface of a recurrent personality type that certainly embodies conflicts but that is certainly not inexplicable. The demonstration of this second thesis is dependent upon a demonstration of the first.

Gordon Ross Smith

The ironic interplay between the images of Caesar the man and Caesar the political figure suggests an important distinction between Brutus and Cassius. The shrewd Cassius sees the conspiracy in terms of individual men, whereas Brutus sees it in terms of principles unfortunately embodied in men. Brutus is not concerned with Caesar the man as Cassius is, but only with "the spirit of Caesar" (Act II, Sc. 1, 167): this is the public Caesar, Caesarism, the principles for which Caesar stands and their potentiality for evil. Brutus considered and rejected the personal argument three separate times in his "orchard" soliloquy (Act II, Sc. 1. 10-12, 19-21, 28-29). For Brutus the conspiracy will destroy in advance the tyranny that Caesar may bring, with its probable suppression of republican liberties. The murder of Caesar the man, no matter what one's personal attachment, is a necessary means to this end. Cassius, on the other hand, emphasizes the infirmities and tyranny of Caesar the man as if all that were needed to right matters in Rome were the death of Caesar; Cassius does not really seem to be at all concerned with the issue of Caesarism. But the course of the dramatic action reverses Brutus' plan and shows its tragic wrongness, for the conspirators are only able to kill the body of Caesar not the spirit.

The murder of Caesar proves to be not a loving sacrifice, but only a fruitless act of butchery, and its bloodiness is stressed as significantly as the murder of Duncan in *Macbeth*. When all is done, only the body of Caesar has been killed, not the spirit, which stays very much alive in Antony and Octavius and wins vengeance in civil strife.

Maurice Charney

Bibliography

Ayres, H. M. "Shakespeare's *Julius Caesar* in the Light of Some Other Versions," *PMLA*, XXV (1910).

Barroll, J. Leeds. "Shakespeare and Roman History." *Modern Language Review*, LIII (1958).

Brewer, D. S. "Brutus' Crime: A Footnote to *Julius Caesar*," *Review of English Studies*, New Series, III (1952).

Breyer, Bernard. *A New Look at Julius Caesar, Essays in Honor of Walter Clyde Curry*. Nashville, Tenn., 1954.

Charlton, H. B. *Shakespearian Tragedy*. Cambridge: Cambridge University Press, 1948; reprinted 1961.

Charney, Maurice. *Shakespeare's Roman Plays*. Cambridge, Mass.: Harvard University Press, 1961.

Coleridge, Samuel Taylor. *Coleridge's Shakespearean Criticism*, T. M. Raysor, ed. Cambridge, Mass.: Harvard University Press, 1930.

Coles, Blanche. *Julius Caesar*. New York: AMS Press, Inc., 1969.

Daiches, David. *Shakespeare: Julius Caesar*. London: Edward Arnold Ltd., 1976.

Dorsch, T. S., ed. *Julius Caesar*. The New Arden Shakespeare, London, 1955.

Foakes, R. A. "An Approach to *Julius Caesar*," *Shakespeare Quarterly*, V (1954).

Granville-Barker, Harley. *Prefaces to Shakespeare*. Princeton: Princeton University Press, 1947, II.

Hirst, David L. *Julius Caesar*. Oxford: Basil Blackwell, 1971.

Hunter, Sir Mark. "Politics and Character in Shakespeare's *Julius Caesar*," *Essays by Divers Hands: Translation of the Royal Society of Literature*, X (1931).

Kirschbaum, Leo. "Shakespeare's Stage Blood and Its Critical Significance," *PMLA*, LXIV (1949).

Kittredge, G. L. "Introduction," *The Tragedy of Julius Caesar*. Boston: Ginn & Co., 1939.

Knight, G. Wilson. *The Imperial Theme*. London: Methuen & Co., 1954; New York: Barnes & Noble, Inc.

Knights, L. C. "Shakespeare and Political Wisdom," *Sewanee Review*, LXI (1953).

MacCallum, M. W. *Shakespeare's Roman Plays and Their Background*. London, 1910.

Phillips, James Emerson Jr. *The State in Shakespeare's Greek and Roman Plays*. New York: Columbia University Press, 1940.

Ribner, Irving. *Patterns in Shakespearian Tragedy*. New York: Barnes & Noble, 1960.

Schanzer, Ernest. "The Problem of *Julius Caesar*," *Shakespeare Quarterly*, (1955).

Schanzer, Ernest. "The Tragedy of Shakespeare's Brutus," *ELH*, XXII (1955).

Smith, Gordon Ross. "Brutus, Virtue, and Will," *Shakespeare Quarterly*, X (1959).

Smith, Warren D. "The Duplicate Revelation of Portia's Death," *Shakespeare Quarterly*, IV (1953).

Spencer, T. J. B. "Shakespeare and the Elizabethan Romans," *Shakespeare Survey* 10 (Cambridge, 1957).

Stewart, J. I. M. *"Julius Caesar* and *Macbeth,"* *Modern Language Review*, XI (1945).

Stirling, Brents. *Unity in Shakespearian Tragedy*. New York: Columbia Univ. Press, 1956.

Van Doren, Mark. *Shakespeare*. New York: Henry Holt & Co., 1939; Doubleday Anchor Books, 1953.

NOTES